Managing Illegal Immigration to the United States
How Effective Is Enforcement?

D1524287

COUNCIL *on*
FOREIGN
RELATIONS

May 2013

Bryan Roberts
Edward Alden
John Whitley

Managing Illegal Immigration to the United States
How Effective Is Enforcement?

The Council on Foreign Relations (CFR) is an independent, nonpartisan membership organization, think tank, and publisher dedicated to being a resource for its members, government officials, business executives, journalists, educators and students, civic and religious leaders, and other interested citizens in order to help them better understand the world and the foreign policy choices facing the United States and other countries. Founded in 1921, CFR carries out its mission by maintaining a diverse membership, with special programs to promote interest and develop expertise in the next generation of foreign policy leaders; convening meetings at its headquarters in New York and in Washington, DC, and other cities where senior government officials, members of Congress, global leaders, and prominent thinkers come together with CFR members to discuss and debate major international issues; supporting a Studies Program that fosters independent research, enabling CFR scholars to produce articles, reports, and books and hold roundtables that analyze foreign policy issues and make concrete policy recommendations; publishing *Foreign Affairs*, the preeminent journal on international affairs and U.S. foreign policy; sponsoring Independent Task Forces that produce reports with both findings and policy prescriptions on the most important foreign policy topics; and providing up-to-date information and analysis about world events and American foreign policy on its website, CFR.org.

The Council on Foreign Relations takes no institutional positions on policy issues and has no affiliation with the U.S. government. All views expressed in its publications and on its website are the sole responsibility of the author or authors.

For further information about CFR or this publication, please write to the Council on Foreign Relations, 58 East 68th Street, New York, NY 10065, or call Communications at 212.434.9888. Visit CFR's website, www.cfr.org.

This report is printed on paper that is FSC® certified by Rainforest Alliance, which promotes environmentally responsible, socially beneficial, and economically viable management of the world's forests.

MIX
Paper from
responsible sources
FSC® C015782

Contents

Acknowledgments

We are immensely grateful to the members of the report's advisory committee, who provided invaluable assistance in shaping the concepts of this paper and offering feedback on an earlier draft. We were incredibly fortunate to be able to draw from the wisdom and experience of some of the foremost academic and government leaders working on issues of border security and enforcement. The group was superbly chaired by Pia Orrenius of the Dallas Federal Reserve, and we especially thank her for her generosity and insights. Other members of the committee were: Jayson Ahern, Frank D. Bean, Rob Bonner, Peter Brownell, Joseph Chang, Mariano-Florentino Cuellar, Marshall Fitz, George Gavrilis, Stephen Heifetz, Antonia Hernandez, Donald Kerwin, Rey Koslowski, Chappell Lawson, Magnus Lofstrom, David A. Martin, Susan F. Martin, Eliseo Medina, Doris M. Meissner, Shannon K. O'Neil ex officio, Rob Quartel, Peter Reuter, Lora L. Ries, Marc Rosenblum, Andrew Selee, David Shirk, Margaret D. Stock, Brian M. White, Madeline Zavodny, and James W. Ziglar. Their feedback improved the paper in numerous ways, but the authors are solely responsible for the content and the views expressed.

CFR Director of Editorial Strategy Anya Schmemann provided helpful feedback, and we appreciate the ongoing support of Director of Studies James M. Lindsay. We would also like to thank Jane McMurrey, Rebecca Strauss, and Ha-Vi Nguyen for initial edits and for their excellent work on the tables and figures in the report; the superb team in Publications, Patricia Dorff, Lia Norton, and Ashley Bregman, for getting it into final shape; and Tricia Miller in Global Communications and Media Relations for support on outreach. Many of the ideas in this paper were shared with committee staff in Congress working on immigration legislation, and we would like to thank Patrick Costello and Mark Collins of CFR's Congress and U.S. Foreign Policy staff for their help in arranging some of those meetings.

Edward Alden would like to thank Mack McLarty, co-chair of the 2009 CFR-sponsored *Independent Task Force on U.S. Immigration Policy*, and other members of the Task Force for their ongoing interest in the issue of measuring border enforcement. John Whitley would like to thank Molly Valdes-Dapena and Gregory Pejic. Bryan Roberts would like to thank the analysts working inside or with the Department of Homeland Security who have sought to make progress in the face of many obstacles.

Finally, this report was made possible by a generous grant from the Bernard and Irene Schwartz Foundation, and we are grateful to them both for their ongoing support of research, publications, and programming at the Council on Foreign Relations.

Bryan Roberts
Edward Alden
John Whitley
May 2013

Acronyms

ADIS	Arrival and Departure Information System
BCC	Border Crossing Card
CBP	Customs and Border Protection
COMPEX	United States Customs Service's Compliance Measurement Exam
DHS	Department of Homeland Security
DOJ	Department of Justice
GAO	Government Accountability Office
GPRA	Government Performance and Results Act
ICE	Immigration and Customs Enforcement
INS	Immigration and Naturalization Service
IRCA	Immigration Reform and Control Act
LAWA	Legal Arizona Worker Act
MMFRP	Mexican Migration Field Research Program
MMP	Mexican Migration Project
NAFTA	North American Free Trade Agreement
OFO	Office of Field Operations
PA&E	Program Analysis and Evaluation
PPP	purchasing power parity
USCG	United States Coast Guard
USBP	United States Border Patrol
US-VISIT	United States Visitor and Immigrant Status Indicator Technology
WDI	World Development Indicators

Introduction

For the past two decades, Congress has vastly increased the resources devoted to immigration enforcement. By every conceivable input measure—the number of Border Patrol agents, miles of fencing, drone and surveillance coverage—the U.S. border with Mexico today should be far more secure than it has ever been. Border Patrol personnel have doubled since 2004 to more than twenty-one thousand, more than 650 miles of fencing have been built, and the border is draped with ground sensors and aerial surveillance. In an effort to deter further illegal migration, the federal government has also ramped up interior enforcement of immigration laws, doubling the number of removals annually over the past decade, mandating the use of employment verification for government contractors, and increasing workplace audits. A recent study by the Migration Policy Institute found that the United States spends more on immigration enforcement, nearly $18 billion in fiscal year (FY) 2012, than on all other federal law enforcement missions combined.[1]

Yet, despite these efforts, the American public remains skeptical about the effectiveness of immigration enforcement. According to a recent survey, nearly two-thirds of Americans believe the border is still not secure.[2] One reason for the skepticism is that the U.S. government has done too little to measure and evaluate its enforcement efforts and has not made public the results of the small amount of analysis that has been done internally. For border enforcement, the Department of Homeland Security (DHS) releases only a single output number: the total arrests, or apprehensions, made by Border Patrol agents of unauthorized crossers in the vicinity of the border. Other important enforcement metrics related to illegal entry at the ports, between the ports, or visa overstays are not reported.

U.S. enforcement has likely discouraged illegal entry. However, such basic questions as the apprehension rate for unauthorized crossers or the estimated number of successful illegal entries cannot be answered simply by counting arrest totals. The lack of more robust data is puzzling, given core DHS missions. Marc Rosenblum of the Congressional Research Service has noted that the first U.S. national border control strategy, drawn up in 1994, when the United States launched what was to become its two-decade-long effort to bolster border enforcement, called for "prevention through deterrence."[3] The 1994 strategy stated, "Although a 100 percent apprehension rate is an unrealistic goal, we believe we can achieve a rate of apprehensions sufficiently high to raise the risk of apprehension to the point that many will consider it futile to continue to attempt illegal entry."[4] Yet, with some slight and intermittent exceptions, DHS has never reported an apprehension rate for the border as a whole or for specific sectors. In the interior, DHS counts the number of removals and the criminal detainees among those removed and releases various statistics related to worksite enforcement. But there has been no effort by DHS to assess empirically the contribution of interior enforcement in deterring illegal migration to the United States. And there has been little effort to weigh the relative value of additional border versus interior enforcement in discouraging illegal migration.

Although the number of illegal crossing attempts has fallen sharply over the past decade, there is little understanding of the role immigration enforcement has played. The Obama administration has not offered, and Congress has failed to insist on, any accountability for the effectiveness of these huge enforcement expenditures. With the U.S. government facing tight budget restrictions, it is imperative that Congress demand cost-effectiveness evaluations from DHS and establish a robust oversight system to evaluate enforcement performance on an ongoing basis. In addition to protecting taxpayer dollars and increasing the effectiveness of enforcement spending, such oversight and accountability would help reassure a skeptical public that the U.S. government is indeed serious about controlling illegal migration.[5] Such an effort begins with understanding the major drivers of illegal immigration to the United States and analyzing the effectiveness of enforcement in deterring illegal migration.

The major conclusions that follow are:

- The U.S. government reports substantial information about inputs into the illegal-immigration enforcement process. The government does not report most outputs, however, nor does it report outcomes.

- While demographic change in Mexico and Central America will reduce the pressure for illegal immigration in the long term, the wage gap that is one of the primary drivers of unauthorized migration has narrowed only slightly. Controlling illegal immigration is therefore likely to remain a significant policy challenge for the United States in the medium-term future.

- It is possible to develop reasonable estimates of the gross inflow of unauthorized migrants and the apprehension rate at the border, and to improve these estimates over time. Based on the best currently available evidence, the apprehension rate along the southwest land border between the ports of entry is likely in the range of 40 to 55 percent. This rate has increased substantially as a result of the recent investments in enforcement.

- The flow of undocumented migrants has decreased substantially. The best estimate available to date (from unpublished research) is that enforcement increases explain approximately one-third of the recent reduction in the flow of undocumented migrants, and economic factors the remainder.

- Analytical work should be carried out by the U.S. government and by outside researchers to understand the effectiveness of interior enforcement, including worksite enforcement, in deterring illegal migration.

- Congress should direct the administration to develop and report a full set of performance measures for immigration enforcement, to systematically undertake program evaluation analysis that measures the effectiveness of individual programs, and to develop an early-warning system to forecast illegal migration trends. Future appropriations should be tied to the development and implementation of such measures.

- The administration should release its enforcement data to outside researchers. DHS should also recruit and support internal researchers, encourage them to work on these issues with academic researchers, and approve their work for public dissemination.

Background

Large-scale migration to the United States from the Western Hemisphere began during World War II. A guest-worker program for Mexican nationals known as the Bracero program was established to provide labor to farms and factories. Demand for workers exceeded the relatively small number of admissions permitted by the Bracero program, which never exceeded sixty-three thousand during the war. Although imperfect and potentially misleading, the number of apprehensions of those attempting illegal entry by the U.S. Border Patrol is often used as a proxy for illegal entry. Apprehensions rose sharply in the mid-1940s (see Figure 1). After the war, the Bracero entry quota was cut sharply, and illegal entry appears to have accelerated dramatically. By the early 1950s, illegal immigration from Mexico had become a significant national issue. After 1954, apprehensions fell to low levels, but after the Bracero program was ended in 1965, they rose rapidly again in the late 1960s and 1970s. In the 1980s and 1990s, they reached record-high levels of 1.2 million per year on average, of whom 97 percent were Mexican nationals. Arrests began to decline in the 2000s, slowly through 2008 and rapidly afterward, so that by 2011, the level was back to that of 1971.

The unauthorized population rose substantially in both absolute numbers and as a percentage of the U.S. population from 1980 to 2007, but it has fallen slightly in subsequent years (see Figure 2).[6] Mexican nationals accounted for 58 percent of the total unauthorized population on average from 1980 to 2011, and nationals from other Latin American countries for 23 percent.[7] Although many unauthorized immigrants entered the United States by crossing the U.S.-Mexico border between ports of entry (legal crossing points), a significant number are also believed to have entered illegally by escaping detection at ports of entry or by overstaying a legal visa. Mexican nationals have accounted for almost all U.S. Border Patrol (USBP) apprehensions, though the number of non-Mexican nationals has been increasing in recent years.

Following the growth in illegal immigration in the 1970s and 1980s, Congress passed the Immigration Reform and Control Act (IRCA) in 1986. IRCA's most important provisions made it illegal for employers to hire unauthorized workers, required employers to verify migration status, and implemented a legalization program that enabled many of the unauthorized population to become legal U.S. residents.[8] Increases in border enforcement resources followed later, first during the mid-1990s and then again during the late 2000s. In the 2000s as well, interior enforcement was sharply increased, including workplace raids, audits, and removal of unauthorized immigrants.

Recent evidence points to a steep fall in new illegal migration over the past five years, coinciding both with the most recent border buildup and with the economic downturn that began in 2007. Many experts, though, remain concerned that illegal flows will resume when the U.S. economy again grows more strongly; indeed, apprehensions in the first half of FY2013 have risen 13 percent from the previous year.

FIGURE 1. U.S. BORDER PATROL ANNUAL APPREHENSIONS AND BRACERO PROGRAM ADMISSIONS

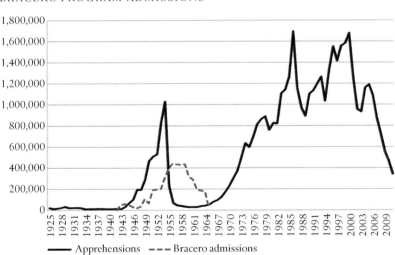

Source: Authors' calculations based on *DHS Yearbook of Immigration Statistics* and CBP.

FIGURE 2. ESTIMATES OF UNAUTHORIZED U.S. POPULATION

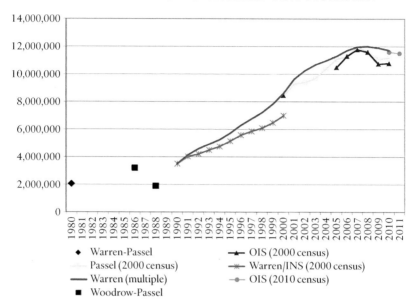

Source: Authors' calculations based on Warren and Passel, "A Count of the Uncountable"; Woodrow and Passel, "Post-IRCA Undocumented Immigration"; Warren and Warren, "Unauthorized Immigration."

Why Do Migrants Come
to the United States Illegally?

Any assessment of border control efforts should begin with some understanding of why migrants choose to come to the United States illegally. Predicting whether the recent downturn in illegal immigration is likely to be transitory or permanent depends in part on whether the perceived costs and benefits of migrating illegally will change in the future.

To simplify, a potential migrant will compare the benefits that can be expected from relocating to the United States with the costs of relocating. Benefits can be economic, such as a better wage or income. Benefits can also include family reunification, improved access to health care and education for the migrant's children, and better police protection and security. Costs include payments associated with travel and relocation—lawyers for legal immigration processing or payments to smugglers for assistance with illegal entry. They also include the dangers of illegal entry, loss of wages and other punishment if an illegal entry attempt results in capture and prosecution, and the challenges of having to leave one's home and of being separated from family and friends. A typical potential migrant will migrate if benefits are believed ex ante to significantly exceed costs.

This calculus fluctuates with the near-term business cycle and hard-to-predict policy shocks such as the North American Free Trade Agreement (NAFTA), which led to a sharp increase in immigration in the mid-1990s. In the short run, as the U.S. economy recovers from the Great Recession, illegal immigration will continue to be relatively low because the demand for unskilled labor will be low. The question for policymakers is what will happen in the medium term, once labor demand has returned to normal, and in the long term, several decades out.[9]

Besides U.S. immigration enforcement, three structural trends have the largest bearing on the cost-benefit migration calculus: the relative wage gap between the sending and receiving countries, the supply of potential migrants from population growth, and the strength of immigrant social networks in the receiving country. Because immigrant social networks are now well established in the United States, relative wages and demographic trends are likely to play the biggest role in driving future illegal immigration pressures.[10]

RELATIVE WAGES IN SOURCE COUNTRIES AND THE UNITED STATES: ANY SIGN OF CONVERGENCE?

The main economic factor influencing migration is the wage gap, or the difference between what a potential migrant can earn in the United States and in the migrant's home country. Differences in average wages for similar workers between developed and developing countries constitute the single largest price distortion remaining in global markets.[11] Given these wage differences, what is surprising is not how much migration takes place in the world but how little. The example of the United States and Mexico is one of the few in modern history where large-scale migration in the presence of a large wage gap has taken place.[12] A critical question for assessing likely future immigration trends is whether the wage gap is narrowing. The best evidence suggests that little convergence is actually occurring, which means that pressures for illegal migration are likely to remain.

In the late 1990s and 2000s, migrant survey data suggested that wage gaps based on actual labor market outcomes in the United States and Mexico were typically equal to seven, if valued at the commercial exchange rate, and four, if valued at the purchasing power parity (PPP) exchange rate, which looks at the relative costs of a standard basket of goods (see Appendix 1 online).[13] These values are consistent with per capita income gaps. Another approach is to use household survey data for the United States and Mexico and compare wage levels for workers with identical observable characteristics, such as education, age, gender, and nationality. Michael Clemens, Claudio Montenegro, and Lant Pritchett estimated wage gaps for many nationalities using U.S. Census data for 2000 and household survey data for other countries for years close to 2000. Their estimate was 2.5 using the PPP exchange rate, which implies a wage gap of 3.9 using the commercial exchange rate.[14] Analysis of the longer-run trend in the U.S.-Mexico wage gap from 1987 to 2001 using household survey data has found little evidence of convergence.[15]

Data on the income gap are available going back much further in time. The income gap can be calculated using the commercial exchange rate for 1960 to 2010 and the PPP exchange rate for 1870 to 2008 (see Figure 3). The PPP income gap has fluctuated between three and four for more than 140 years, and the graph makes it clear that no evidence of convergence exists.[16] The income gap valued at the commercial exchange rate has fallen from eight in the early 1960s to between five and six in the late 2000s.[17] But even if the linear trend evident in this ratio between 1960 and 2010 is extrapolated forward, the gap will still be above three in 2075.[18]

The incentives that a wage gap equal to three creates for migration are powerful, particularly when the costs of migrating are relatively low. Take, for example, a case in which a migrant can earn $5,000 per year in Mexico and $15,000 in the United States and has to pay a smuggling cost of $3,000 for an illegal trip into the United States. If the migrant makes one trip home a year, then in one year he or she will earn $7,000 more in the United States than in Mexico after subtracting the smuggling cost. If he or she is a circular migrant and goes back and forth ten times over the course of a decade, then accumulated extra earnings, net of smuggling costs, equal $70,000. This amount of money might not seem particularly large to Americans, but it reflects an extraordinary opportunity that many people would find irresistible. To better highlight the implications of such a wage gap, consider two scenarios in which the United States is the home country and an unspecified X is the destination country, and a wage gap and relative smuggling cost are applied to U.S. earnings (see Table 1). In a case where one could earn $50,000 in the United States but triple that in country X, over a decade of circular migration, one could accumulate $700,000 in net extra earnings. In a case where one could earn $150,000 in the United States, a decade of accumulated net extra earnings would equal $2.1 million. These examples illustrate that in the presence of a wage gap equal to three, only a relatively few years of working in the destination country could finance a comfortable retirement in the home country.[19]

Income is not the only determinant of the quality of life, which is also potentially influenced by the rate of poverty and access to basic services in the areas of health, sanitation, and nutrition. These noneconomic indicators generally have been improving in Mexico, El Salvador, and Guatemala in recent decades. Poverty rates also generally fell between 1984 and 2010.

FIGURE 3. U.S. TO MEXICAN INCOME

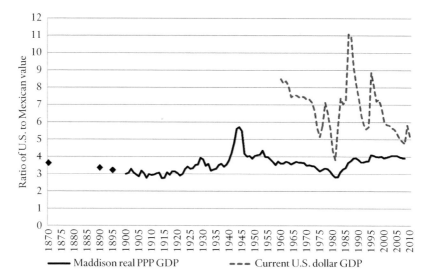

Source: Authors' calculations based on Angus Maddison, *Contours of the World Economy, 1–2030 AD* (Oxford: Oxford University Press, 2007) and World Development Indicators (WDI) databank.

Mexico is, of course, not the only significant major source country for migrants to the United States. Appendix 2 online reviews wage gap data for Central American countries, which provide the highest numbers of illegal immigrants after Mexico.

BABY BOOMS HAVE BECOME BABY BUSTS: DEMOGRAPHIC TRENDS IN SOURCE COUNTRIES

Wage gaps between the United States and major source countries for unauthorized immigrants have been substantial since at least 1920, and, in the case of Mexico, since at least 1870, but true mass migration from these countries did not begin until after World War II. One big reason was a baby boom in Mexico and Central America, causing a spike in the supply of potential migrants.

If birthrates are high and most children survive to adulthood, the number of young people entering the labor force fifteen to twenty

TABLE 1. THE WAGE GAP IN PERSPECTIVE

	Mexico to United States	United States to Country X	
		Typical Salary	High Salary
Average annual migrant earnings in destination country	$15,000	$150,000	$450,000
Average annual migrant earnings in home country	$5,000	$50,000	$150,000
Ratio	3	3	3
Annual smuggling cost paid	$3,000	$30,000	$90,000
Percent of earnings in destination country	20	20	20
Accumulated extra gross earnings net of smuggling cost over			
1 year	$7,000	$70,000	$210,000
2 years	$14,000	$140,000	$420,000
5 years	$35,000	$350,000	$1,050,000
10 years	$70,000	$700,000	$2,100,000

Source: Authors' assumptions based on review of data from Mexican Migration Project Survey; Mexican Migration Field Research Project Survey; Cornelius et al., *Migration from the Mexican Mixteca*; Cornelius et al., *Four Generations of Norteños*; Cornelius et al., *Mexican Migration and the U.S. Economic Crisis*.

years later will increase dramatically. The total fertility rate—the average number of children born to each woman—in Mexico, El Salvador, Guatemala, and Honduras was between six and eight from the 1950s through the 1970s (see Figure 4). This baby boom caused a subsequent increase in these countries' workforces from the late 1960s to the 1990s. But fertility in these countries has since fallen dramatically, and is currently similar to the level of the United States.[20]

This fall in fertility in recent decades, along with slower growing workforces, may have contributed to the decline in illegal migration in the 2000s (see Figure 5). Young Mexican and Central American men make up the majority of illegal entry apprehensions, and, at least until 1990, the number of apprehensions could be predicted from the size of the young male population in Mexico and Central America.[21]

Beginning in the mid-1990s, however, the historic link between population and apprehension trends loosened, with apprehensions rising above and then falling below the trend. Apprehensions were unusually high in the late 1990s, probably due to special events in the mid-1990s, such as the 1994 peso crisis and NAFTA, which reduced agricultural employment in Mexico. Apprehensions then fell substantially in the late 2000s, probably because of the Great Recession, improved economic outcomes in Mexico, intensified enforcement in the United States, and increased use of temporary-worker programs such as the H-2A farmworker visa.[22]

If the historic relationship between population and apprehension variables resumes, barring other developments, population trends suggest that a rebound in illegal inflow is to be expected in the medium term. The primary source population for illegal immigration—young

FIGURE 4. TOTAL FERTILITY RATES

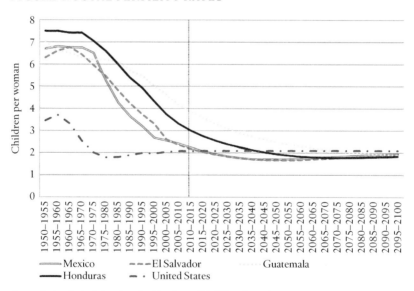

Source: Authors' calculations based on Database of World Population Prospect: 2010 Revision; UN Population Division of the Department of Economic and Social Affairs.

FIGURE 5. APPREHENSIONS OF MALE YOUTH FROM MEXICO AND
CENTRAL AMERICA

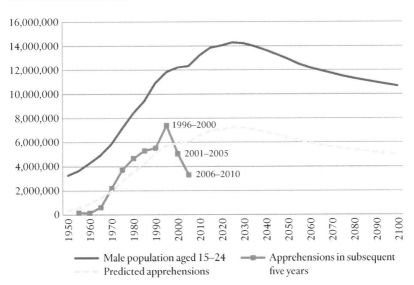

Source: Authors' calculations based on Database of World Population Prospects: 2010 Revision; UN Population Division of Economic and Social Affairs; and DHS.

Mexican and Central American men—is projected to continue growing somewhat through 2030 and then begin to decline.

PROSPECTS FOR STRUCTURAL FACTORS INFLUENCING THE LEVEL OF IMMIGRATION

These structural factors should be considered in developing immigration reform proposals. If the recent downturn in illegal immigration is likely to continue because of these trends, then a legalization plan for the existing resident population of unauthorized immigrants is unlikely to encourage additional future illegal immigration. Alternatively, if the recent downturn is expected to be short-lived and long-term structural factors will drive a return to higher levels of attempted illegal entry, then any reform without a plan to counter this resurgence could simply reprise the 1986 IRCA. That legislation did little to control illegal immigration and possibly made it worse through the incentive effects of the legalization provision.

The likely effect of structural trends on the future level of illegal immigration is mixed:

- Differentials in wages and living standards between the United States and major source countries have not converged significantly since 1870. Any future convergence is likely to affect migration only in the long term. A significant gap capable of inducing migration is likely to endure for many decades.

- Growth in potential-migrant populations in the major source countries has been slowing since the 1980s, but these populations are not projected to start falling in absolute numbers until roughly 2030.

Unless a strong recovery in housing construction emerges in the near term, migrant inflows are unlikely to grow significantly in the short run. Once economic recovery is on a solid footing and labor demand has fully recovered, the potential for resurgence in migrant inflows is real. Its magnitude will be determined primarily by the degree that unskilled labor is demanded in a post-recovery economy and the recent U.S. enforcement buildup is sustained. In the long run, demand to migrate to the United States from these countries is likely to abate as the size of potential-migrant populations fall.

The United Nations develops projections of net migration for every country in the world, though their methodology could be more accurate (see Figure 6). Net emigration from Mexico was projected to remain significant in coming decades. However, these projections may not take into account recent evidence on the degree of the fall in net emigration from Mexico. This sudden change suggests that more detailed empirical modeling of these trends is needed, particularly analysis that distinguishes between legal and illegal flows.

FIGURE 6. NET EMIGRANTS FROM PRIMARY SOURCE COUNTRIES

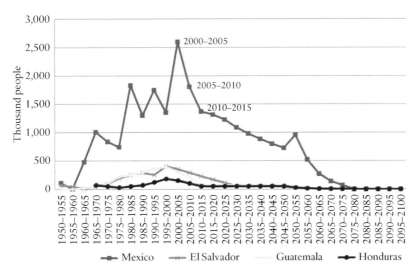

Source: Authors' calculations based on Database of World Population Prospects: 2010 Revision; UN Population Division of Economic and Social Affairs.

What Prevents Migrants From Coming to the United States Illegally?

Immigrants to the United States have a choice between legal and illegal pathways. The decision is based on the relative costs and benefits of the two pathways. When a legal option is available (such as a family sponsor, a skilled work visa such as the H-1B or TN, or a temporary work visa such as the H2A or H2B) and the pathway functions efficiently, a legal route will generally be preferred. But if a legal pathway is not available, or is too cumbersome or costly, an illegal pathway may become the preferred avenue. In considering the risks involved with an illegal pathway, the effectiveness of U.S. enforcement, both at the border and in the interior, may affect the choices that would-be migrants make. This section examines U.S. immigration enforcement activities and the effect they have on illegal immigration.

ILLEGAL IMMIGRATION AND ENFORCEMENT

Enforcement increases the costs and reduces the benefits of entering the United States illegally. Border enforcement increases the chance that someone attempting illegal entry will be caught and subjected to punishment. Interior enforcement increases the chance that someone who has successfully entered will be either unable to find paying work or caught and subjected to punishment. Enforcement also creates deterrence, which can be broken down into two elements. First, specific deterrence focuses on an individual committing a crime; arresting and punishing the individual may prevent him from committing another crime. Second, general or indirect deterrence dissuades potential criminals from committing a crime in the first place. In border enforcement, these elements are called *at-the-border* deterrence (deterring an immigrant from another attempted illegal border crossing, what is known as recidivism) and *behind-the-border* deterrence (causing a potential immigrant to not to attempt illegal migration in the first place).

Enforcement against illegal immigration is implemented by a complex network of U.S. federal agencies. Apprehending and removing unauthorized immigrants is the responsibility of the Department of Homeland Security (DHS) and its subordinate components, Immigration and Customs Enforcement (ICE), Customs and Border Protection (CBP), and the United States Coast Guard (USCG). The Department of Justice (DOJ) has responsibility for prosecuting and sentencing those who are apprehended and brought to trial. Local law enforcement agencies also cooperate with federal agencies and play a role in enforcement. The basic framework in which illegal immigration occurs can be simply illustrated in a diagram (see Figure 7).

Visitors and immigrants are permitted to enter the United States legally at ports of entry, including airports, seaports, and land ports on the borders with Mexico and Canada. Enforcement at ports of entry includes document and vehicle inspection by CBP officers. Illegal immigration can occur at the ports of entry by the migrant presenting false entry documentation or by evading the screening process (for example,

FIGURE 7. ILLEGAL IMMIGRATION FRAMEWORK

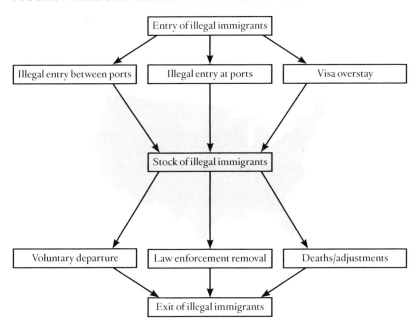

Source: Authors' schematic based on DHS, CBP, ICE, and USCG data.

in the trunk of a car). The U.S. Border Patrol, a component of CBP, operates exclusively between ports of entry, where any attempt to enter is by definition illegal. The USCG operates at sea and on the coasts and is responsible for most enforcement in the maritime domain. ICE operates primarily in the interior of the United States. An immigrant who enters legally and then becomes illegal by violating the conditions of the visa falls under the jurisdiction of ICE. All of these organizations collect data through their own information systems and report selected data on their activities independently of each other.

ENFORCEMENT RESOURCES: HOW MUCH IS DEPLOYED TODAY?

These organizations have each seen a big increase in funding and manpower over the past two decades. At the ports of entry, enforcement is carried out by CBP's Office of Field Operations (OFO). CBP currently has about twenty-two thousand officers. The U.S. Border Patrol manages between the ports of entry enforcement on land and some maritime portions of the Gulf of Mexico. The bulk of the maritime domain is the responsibility of the USCG. The Border Patrol deploys a combination of agents, tactical infrastructure (such as pedestrian and vehicle fencing), and technology. Border Patrol manpower more than doubled in the late 1990s and then again in the late 2000s (see Figure 8). Fencing grew somewhat in the 1990s and then dramatically, starting in 2006. Currently 651 miles of the 1,969-mile southwest border are fenced, most in California and Arizona. The Border Patrol also makes use of many types of infrastructure and equipment, including sensors, night-vision equipment, camera towers, patrol vehicles, river patrol boats, manned and unmanned aerial vehicles, and horses. After decades of underfunding, the Border Patrol now enjoys access to resources that better correspond to the demands of its missions.[23] Appropriations for the Border Patrol have increased by roughly 750 percent since 1989.[24]

ICE, which is responsible for interior enforcement, oversees a vast network of detention facilities and private prisons, and coordinates the arrest and removal of unauthorized immigrants. Since FY1990, the number of annual removals has grown from 30,000 to 188,000 in FY2000 to more than 400,000 in FY2012. ICE funding rose by 87 percent, from $3.1 billion in FY2005 to $5.9 billion in FY2012. The agency has also expanded efforts to investigate and penalize employers who hire unauthorized immigrant workers. Since January 2009, ICE has carried out more than eight thousand workplace audits, barred 726 companies from receiving federal contracts, and imposed nearly $90 million in fines against employers.[25]

Tracking resources used to enforce immigration laws is more straightforward than measuring the outputs those resources are intended to produce. The United States has spent a great deal on immigration enforcement—nearly $220 billion since the passage of the 1986 IRCA, according to the Migration Policy Institute report. The performance of an organization, however, cannot be assessed on the basis of expenditures. If that were the case, the private-sector company with the highest costs would be judged the most successful, regardless of profits. The performance of the illegal-immigration enforcement system should instead be assessed on the degree to which it has successfully prevented illegal entry into the United States.

FIGURE 8. U.S. BORDER PATROL MANPOWER AND FENCE RESOURCES

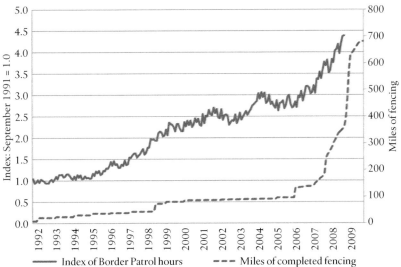

Source: Authors' calculations based on DHS data; Borger, Hanson, and Roberts, "The Decision to Emigrate from Mexico."

MEASURING ILLEGAL IMMIGRATION OUTCOMES AT THE BORDER: WHAT DO WE KNOW?

The U.S. government has long reported apprehensions by the Border Patrol as a measure of enforcement performance.But apprehensions are not a satisfactory measure of the outcome that the U.S. public cares most about, which is the number of unauthorized migrants who escape detection and enter the United States successfully.[26] The two primary enforcement variables that affect this gross inflow are the chances of being caught (the apprehension rate) and the consequences of being caught. Together, these variables determine the expected enforcement-related cost of immigrating illegally, which in turn affects the number of attempted illegal entries, the number of successful entries, and the degree of deterrence of illegal entry attempts. The probability of apprehension and gross inflow can be measured for specific sites of attempted entry: between land ports of entry, at land ports of entry, and through sea routes.

PROBABILITY OF APPREHENSION AND GROSS INFLOW BETWEEN LAND PORTS OF ENTRY

Three relatively low-cost methods can be used to measure gross inflow and apprehension rates between ports of entry: migrant surveys, recidivism analysis, and known-flow data (for more detail, see Appendix 3 online). Using each of these, the probability of apprehension has risen in the 2000s and the number of successful entries between land ports of entry on the southwest border has fallen sharply.

Migrant surveys ask those who have attempted illegal entry how many times they were apprehended on a particular trip and whether they ultimately succeeded or gave up their attempt. These data can provide a direct estimate of the probability of apprehension and the degree of at-the-border deterrence, but the currently available surveys are not timely enough and are subject to other limitations.[27] Migrant surveys collect data on attempted crossings between and at the ports of entry, so that probability of apprehension estimates derived from their data are a weighted average of the probability of apprehension between ports and at ports.[28] Migrant surveys also collect data only on attempted crossings made by Mexican nationals. Data from two migrant surveys are available that permit estimating the probability of apprehension: the Mexican Migration Project (MMP) and the Mexican Migration Field Research Program (MMFRP).

Recidivism analysis is possible because the Border Patrol has captured fingerprints of those apprehended in illegal crossings for more than a decade, so those caught multiple times attempting illegal entry can be identified. Under certain assumptions, this analysis allows for accurate estimates of the apprehension rate. If at-the-border deterrence equals zero—meaning that everyone returned to Mexico tries again—then the probability of apprehension equals the ratio of recidivist apprehensions (that is, all apprehensions after the first) to total apprehensions. The difficulty, however, is that an unknown percentage of those apprehended and returned to Mexico will give up and go home rather than trying to enter again. Estimates of the probability of apprehension developed using recidivism analysis are for Mexican nationals only.[29]

Finally, known-flow data—the number of people estimated to have attempted illegal entry—are based on sector-by-sector observations by the Border Patrol. Each sector has long kept such records, which include estimates of the number of people who successfully evade the Border Patrol (known as got-aways) or are observed retreating to Mexico after contact with the Border Patrol (known as turn-backs). The difficulty here is that some percentage of illegal migrants will successfully enter the United States unobserved by the Border Patrol.

Evidence from the migrant surveys suggests that the probability of apprehension of Mexican nationals rose in the 2000s, and in the last years of the decade had reached roughly 50 to 60 percent (see Figure 9). In other words, on any given attempt, the likelihood of being caught was one in two. Similar results have been suggested by a recent test over the Arizona desert by DHS using observations from airborne radar.[30] The recidivism-based estimates do not show a sustained rise in the probability of apprehension, but the outcome depends heavily on assumptions about deterrence. If a higher percentage of migrants is giving up after being apprehended the first time, then recidivist analysis would suggest that the apprehension rate has increased. That is likely what has taken place over the past decade. Evidence from migrant surveys suggests that the rate of at-the-border deterrence was rising in the 2000s, so that over the 2000s the true probability of apprehension was moving from the short dotted line to the short dashed line in Figure 9. DHS began to impose more significant consequences, including jail sentences, on a growing number of those caught at the border starting in the late 2000s, which may also have discouraged migrants from making multiple entry attempts. Finally, known-flow data also suggest that the probability of apprehension was rising from 2006 to 2011, and was significantly higher than the level suggested by the other methodologies.[31]

Given the available evidence, a conservative lower bound for the probability of apprehension in recent years is 40 percent and a conservative upper bound is 55 percent. These values are significantly higher than the 30 percent that many observers have traditionally cited, including Border Patrol officials, and are much higher than the 10 percent or 20 percent typically assumed by those who believe the border is highly porous.[32]

The gross inflow of unauthorized Mexican-national immigrants, or the number of successful entries, was reduced sharply in the 2000s (see Figure 10).[33] Before the 2000s, the two migrant surveys give wildly different estimates.[34] However, in the 2000s, all estimates show a significant fall in the number of successful entries. By 2009–2010, all estimates of successful entries were below 500,000 annually.[35] Differences between the migrant survey and recidivism estimates are remarkably small. All of these estimates are, however, roughly 50 percent higher than the number of got-aways recorded by the Border Patrol using known-flow methodology.

AT-THE-BORDER DETERRENCE BETWEEN LAND PORTS OF ENTRY

The rate of at-the-border deterrence, or the chance that someone will give up trying to enter illegally after being caught, has also risen during the 2000s. Estimates of this deterrence rate for Mexican nationals can be made using the MMP and MMFRP migrant surveys. Although an at-the-border deterrence rate of less than 1 percent was observed in MMP data before the 2000s, the rate rose to roughly 15 percent from 2008 to 2010 (see Appendix 3 online).[36] Data from the MMFRP survey suggest that the rate was between 1 and 8 percent before 2008.

FIGURE 9. PROBABILITY OF APPREHENSION ESTIMATES BETWEEN PORTS OF ENTRY

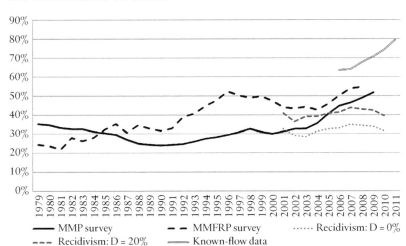

Source: Authors' calculations based on MMP, MMFRP, and GAO data (see Appendix 3 at www.cfr.org/illegal_immigration_report).

FIGURE 10. ESTIMATES OF SUCCESSFUL BETWEEN-PORT LAND ENTRIES

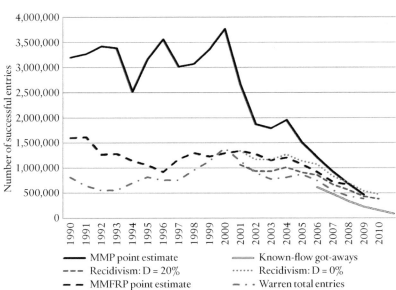

Source: Authors' calculations based on DHS , MMP, and MMFRP data and Warren, 2013.

PROBABILITY OF APPREHENSION AND GROSS INFLOW AT PORTS OF ENTRY

Available evidence on illegal entry at ports of entry is scarce and does not permit definitive conclusions (see Appendix 3 online). Ports of entry are managed by the Office of Field Operations (OFO) of CBP. Although OFO has collected data on apprehensions since 2004, it is not clear that all attempts at illegal entry that are detected and thwarted are included in apprehensions data.[37] The probability of apprehension could presumably be estimated using data from the Customs Service's Compliance Measurement Exam (COMPEX) program of randomized secondary inspections of passenger vehicles that OFO implements at ports of entry. Data are now available on the total number of vehicles and passengers processed at individual ports, permitting estimation of gross inflow. It is not clear whether such estimates have ever been developed by DHS.[38]

The only evidence on illegal entry at land ports on the southern border comes from the MMFRP migrant survey, which suggests that roughly 20 percent of illegal entries by Mexican nationals may have been attempted at land ports in the 2000s.[39] Not accounting for this flow may thus lead to a significant underestimate of gross inflow. Given that DHS completely controls the port environment, it should be straightforward to collect data that permit estimating the size of this inflow. It is true that OFO faces an unusual situation: unlike the Border Patrol, which manages territory through which all entry attempts are illegal, OFO manages ports of entry dominated by large flows of legal entrants, and deals with the challenging mission combination of both preventing illegal entry and facilitating legal flows.[40] The enormous workload that OFO officers face at busy ports of entry may have made data collection and analysis a secondary priority. However, given that randomized sampling and other data collection methods can be implemented at the ports of entry, and that OFO data systems have improved substantially in recent years, estimating illegal inflow at the ports should be possible.

PROBABILITY OF APPREHENSION AT SEA

The one agency of the U.S. government that has officially reported an apprehension or interdiction rate of illegal immigrants is the U.S. Coast Guard, which reported the probability of interdiction of illegal immigrants who attempted to enter the United States by sea from 1995 to 2009. These estimates were based on measures of known flow. USCG initially reported a measure based not only on the number of migrants who were interdicted or successfully entered but also on the number of potential illegal migrants in source countries.[41] A new measure was reported in 2007–2009 that was the ratio of actual interdictions to the estimate of known flow. This interdiction rate was roughly 70 percent on average in this period. In 2010, DHS stopped reporting this rate. It is not clear whether USCG and the interagency process that supported it have continued to make these estimates.[42] The number of successful illegal entries by sea has never been reported publicly, though estimates clearly exist, and they are likely to be small in the context of overall illegal inflows.

MEASURING ILLEGAL IMMIGRATION OUTCOMES IN THE INTERIOR: WHAT DO WE KNOW?

The most important outcomes related to illegal immigration in the interior of the United States are the size of the resident unauthorized immigrant population and of its subcomponents, including (among others) undocumented immigrants in the workforce and those who entered through visa overstay. Interior enforcement is carried out through worksite enforcement (such as worksite raids, audits of companies' efforts to document immigration status before employment, and federal oversight through the E-Verify program), cooperation with local law enforcement to identify unauthorized immigrants, and other activities.

UNAUTHORIZED POPULATION ESTIMATES

Estimates of the total size of the unauthorized immigrant population also suggest a sharp slowing in illegal entries over the past decade. The size was a source of controversy for many years. Before the 1980s, no estimates based on rigorous analysis of population and immigration records were available. As illegal immigration grew in the 1970s and public concern intensified, the Immigration and Naturalization Service (INS) sponsored a project based on a "Delphi technique," which averaged individual speculative assessments and estimated the

unauthorized population at 8.2 million in 1975. INS subsequently lowered its estimate to roughly 6 million and then became reluctant to cite
any number. By the mid-1980s, the first estimate based on residual
methodology was made by Jeffrey Passel of the Census Bureau and
Robert Warren of the INS. Passel, Warren, and their colleagues continued through the 1990s and 2000s to make these estimates, which
are now well known and enjoy widespread credibility.[43]

A particularly useful set of annual estimates has been provided by
Robert Warren and John Robert Warren for 1990 through 2010. For
the United States as a whole, entries—that is, gross inflow—peaked
in 2000, fell significantly from 2001 through 2003, stabilized in 2004
and 2005, and fell significantly in every year after 2005 (see Table 2).
Exits have grown fairly steadily over the entire period, but the change in
why people left tells an important story. Voluntary emigration did not
increase significantly through 2009, but DHS removals rose steadily
over the entire period, as did the odds of an average unauthorized resident being removed.[44] However, the probability of removal was still
only 1.4 percent in 2009, suggesting that the "average" unauthorized
immigrant faced a low likelihood of deportation.

Although the usefulness of a full accounting of stocks and flows for
analysis and policymaking has been discussed in the past, no organized
and systematic effort has ever been made by the U.S. government to
undertake one. As demonstrated by a 1993 GAO report, the government was aware many years ago of the need for such an accounting and
had begun to take steps, but this effort was never consummated. Only
recent efforts outside the government have made progress toward this
goal. In addition to the Warren and Warren study, a 2012 Pew Hispanic
Center report used various data sources to estimate gross inflow, gross
outflow, net migration, and population stocks for Mexico-U.S. migration, including both legal and illegal stocks and flows. It found that net
migration from Mexico to the United States was roughly zero from
2005 to 2010. The residual methodology is subject to several sources
of uncertainty that are described transparently by analysts who have
implemented it.[45] Perhaps the single most important issue is the degree
to which the number of those born in foreign countries but living in the
United States is undercounted in household surveys and the decennial
census. Those making residual estimates assume that this population is
undercounted by 10 to 15 percent.[46]

CONSISTENCY AMONG ESTIMATES
OF FLOWS AND STOCKS

Comparing total inflow estimates from migrant surveys, recidivism analysis, known-flow data, and residual methodology shows some variation by method in overall levels, but the amount of variation has narrowed over time, and all methods show the same downward trend (see Figure 10). Estimates based on migrant surveys and recidivism analysis are for gross inflow of Mexican nationals only between ports of entry on the southwest border, and estimates based on known-flow data are for entries of all nationals between ports of entry on the southwest border. These estimates are thus for only one component of total inflow. The Warren residual-based estimates, however, include inflow of all nationalities in all domains (between the ports, at the ports, and through visa overstay) and should thus be higher than the estimates based on the other methodologies. However, the residual estimates are actually somewhat less than the survey- and recidivism-based estimates, and exceed only the known-flow estimates. Circular migration helps reconcile the discrepancy to some extent, because some of those entering the United States illegally leave the same year; they will be included in migrant surveys and recidivism analysis but presumably not in the residual approach. It may also be that the probability of apprehension is higher than suggested by migrant survey data and recidivism analysis. Such discrepancies suggest that an effort needs to be made to develop estimates of all major stocks and flows to improve accuracy. These discrepancies were not very large in the late 2000s, which suggests that it should be possible to reconcile them and have a complete picture of illegal immigration stocks and flows.

CONSEQUENCES OF GETTING CAUGHT

Deterrence is likely to increase not only as the probability of getting caught increases but also as consequences become more severe. The danger of illegal border crossings has clearly increased over the past two decades, and in recent years the Border Patrol has begun imposing more serious consequences, including jail time, on apprehended border crossers. However, DHS has not yet presented any data showing whether these consequence programs have increased deterrence and reduced recidivism.

TABLE 2. UNAUTHORIZED POPULATION AND COMPONENTS OF CHANGE

	Population on January 1	Net Change	Entries	Exits					Memo: Chance of Being Removed
				Total	Voluntarily Emigrated	Adjusted to Lawful Status	Removed by DHS	Died	
1990	3,500,000	634,935	815,876	180,941	102,648	37,883	25,369	15,041	0.7%
1991	4,134,935	451,657	648,602	196,945	115,922	35,290	28,568	17,165	0.7%
1992	4,586,592	338,841	558,601	219,760	124,179	42,925	33,921	18,735	0.7%
1993	4,925,433	327,496	556,605	229,109	130,175	44,870	34,023	20,041	0.7%
1994	5,252,929	467,097	700,030	232,933	138,038	38,392	34,921	21,582	0.6%
1995	5,720,026	570,626	821,533	250,907	149,624	41,900	35,765	23,618	0.6%
1996	6,290,652	472,185	755,784	283,599	161,052	55,428	41,426	25,693	0.6%
1997	6,762,837	447,625	758,703	311,078	170,283	54,319	58,954	27,522	0.8%
1998	7,210,462	616,056	953,591	337,535	181,664	61,448	64,797	29,626	0.9%
1999	7,826,518	773,481	1,131,520	358,039	197,808	60,393	65,287	34,551	0.8%

	Population on January 1	Net Change	Entries	Total	Voluntarily Emigrated	Adjusted to Lawful Status	Removed by DHS	Died	Memo: Chance of Being Removed
						Exits			
2000	8,599,999	1,020,484	1,389,322	368,838	197,784	72,621	65,279	33,154	0.7%
2001	9,620,483	638,197	1,145,813	507,616	223,171	176,169	71,191	37,085	0.7%
2002	10,258,680	433,518	906,295	472,777	237,468	114,927	80,836	39,546	0.8%
2003	10,692,198	285,752	779,187	493,435	244,470	119,709	88,033	41,223	0.8%
2004	10,977,950	338,848	812,516	473,668	246,684	84,288	100,363	42,333	0.9%
2005	11,316,798	397,498	873,134	475,636	250,187	79,037	102,764	43,648	0.9%
2006	11,714,296	266,996	749,421	482,425	255,867	64,200	117,171	45,187	1.0%
2007	11,981,292	27,212	558,276	531,064	257,585	94,064	133,190	46,225	1.1%
2008	12,008,504	-109,690	439,496	549,186	252,281	100,485	150,079	46,341	1.3%
2009	11,898,814	-173,804	384,314	558,118	243,319	104,029	164,839	45,931	1.4%
2010	11,725,010								

Source: Warren and Warren, "Unauthorized Immigration," table A2.

For many decades, most of those caught entering illegally faced little or no penalty. Most Mexican nationals were granted "voluntary return," in which they were sent across the border to places close to where the attempt had taken place. Most non-Mexican nationals were released into the United States after being assigned a court date at which the majority failed to appear.[47]

These policies began to change in the mid-2000s: non-Mexican nationals were detained, jailed, and flown to their home country rather than being subjected to "catch and release," which significantly increased the cost of being apprehended. In the late 2000s, the Border Patrol also began to apply various "consequence programs" to an increasing proportion of Mexican nationals. These consequences range from an appearance at a "quick court" at a Border Patrol office to being repatriated into the interior of Mexico to serving jail time under Operation Streamline. The results of these programs are being tracked through analysis of recidivism rates, to see whether individuals who face these consequences are less likely to reattempt illegal entry. Recidivism rates for consequence programs are reportedly to be published in a new study by the Congressional Research Service.

Those apprehended today certainly face a different consequence environment than in the pre-2005 era. Nonetheless, DHS has not released adequate data to show how many of those apprehended are subjected to consequences as opposed to voluntary return. DHS has recently provided data on the number of those deemed inadmissible to the United States at ports of entry and those apprehended by ICE.[48] DHS has also long provided data on those subjected to formal removal proceedings and voluntary return (see Table 3). Those subjected to removal and return are not sorted by whether they were apprehended by the Border Patrol, apprehended by ICE, or not admitted at a port of entry. It is thus not possible to determine the percentage of those apprehended by the Border Patrol who were subjected to a consequence, which presumably means being classified as a removal rather than returned voluntarily.

It is possible to obtain ratios from available data to approximate the percentage of apprehensions subjected to a consequence (see Table 3). One ratio assumes that all returns were those apprehended by Border Patrol (row E divided by row B). This overestimates the true percentage, because some inadmissibles (perhaps most) are returns, and even some ICE apprehensions are returns (for example, in some cases where the person has not committed a crime and is willing to pay for his or her

TABLE 3. APPREHENSIONS, INADMISSIBLES, REMOVALS, AND RETURNS

		2005	2006	2007	2008	2009	2010	2011
A	Apprehensions and Inadmissibles	1,542,218	1,414,023	1,162,698	1,266,636	1,094,268	981,732	853,867
B	U.S. Border Patrol apprehensions	1,189,075	1,089,092	876,704	723,825	556,041	463,382	340,252
C	Inadmissibles	251,109	207,610	202,025	222,788	224,402	229,403	212,234
	ICE apprehensions	102,034	117,321	83,969	320,023	313,825	288,947	301,381
D	Removals	246,431	280,974	319,382	359,795	393,457	385,100	391,953
	U.S. Border Patrol	NR	NR	NR	NR	NR	NR	NR
	Inadmissibles	NR	NR	NR	NR	NR	NR	NR
	ICE	NR	NR	NR	NR	NR	NR	NR
E	Returns	1,096,920	1,043,381	891,390	811,263	584,436	475,613	323,542
	U.S. Border Patrol	NR	NR	NR	NR	NR	NR	NR
	Inadmissibles	NR	NR	NR	NR	NR	NR	NR
	ICE	NR	NR	NR	NR	NR	NR	NR
	Memo							
	E/B	92%	96%	102%	112%	105%	103%	95%
	E/(B+C)	76%	80%	83%	86%	75%	69%	59%
	(D+E)/A	87%	94%	104%	92%	89%	88%	84%

*NR indicates not reported.

Source: Authors' calculations based on 2011 DHS Yearbook of Immigration Statistics.

return home). This ratio suggests no significant change in the percentage subjected to consequences.[49] An alternative approximation is the ratio of total returns to Border Patrol apprehensions and inadmissibles (row E divided by row B plus row C).[50] This ratio does show a significant drop from 2008 to 2011, suggesting that an increasing percentage of Border Patrol apprehensions were being subjected to consequences.

It is remarkable that DHS has not published data on apprehensions and inadmissibles by whether they were removed, returned, or sent into another status (for example, incarcerated in the United States). Since these data have not been made public, it is impossible to know with any confidence whether an increasing percentage of those apprehended by Border Patrol have been subjected to consequences rather than voluntarily returned. The lack of such data and inconsistencies between data published by different DHS offices are more deeply problematic. After reviewing enforcement-related data published in the *DHS Yearbook of Immigration Statistics*, Steve Redburn, Peter Reuter, and Malay Majmundar conclude in a 2011 report that

> The differences between data provided to the committee by the DHS component agencies and the data published in the Yearbook raise questions about the completeness of information that government agencies and the public use to estimate immigration flows and, therefore, about the ability of congressional and other policy makers to accurately estimate resource requirements for components of the immigration enforcement system.[51]

Finally, migrant surveys suggest that the conflict among Mexican drug cartels, and between these cartels and the Mexican state during the second half of the 2000s, which has increased violence in the border regions, has also played an increasingly significant role in deterring illegal migration.[52]

VISA OVERSTAY ESTIMATES

Individuals who come to the United State on legal visas, or through the visa waiver program, and then fail to return home as required are thought to make up a significant portion of unauthorized immigrants, perhaps 40 percent. Recent estimates suggest, however, that the number of new overstayers has dropped sharply in the past decade. DHS has also significantly improved its capacity to identify visa overstayers using entry and exit data, and has promised to report these results to Congress by the end of the 2013 calendar year.

The first attempt to estimate the stock or flow associated with visa overstayers was produced by Robert Warren for the 1985 to 1988 period.[53] Arrival stubs for the paper form that all visa travelers entering the United States are required to complete, the I-94 form, were matched to departure stubs from the same form. Arrival stubs lacking a match were designated as apparent overstays, and a correction factor was applied to control for system error, such as an incomplete collection of departure stubs. Warren subsequently developed estimates of the stock of visa overstayers for later years.[54] In 1997, the last year he implemented the stub-matching approach, Warren found that of the estimated 5 million unauthorized migrants resident in the United States, 41 percent (2.1 million) were visa overstayers. The U.S. government has not published any updated estimates based on direct inspection of entry and exit records since 1996. DHS published estimates for 2000 in which visa overstayers were 33 percent of the unauthorized population.[55] In 2006, Pew Hispanic Center updated Warren's estimates up to 2005 by taking estimates of the proportion of unauthorized resident immigrants who were visa overstayers in 1996 and projecting them forward, assuming that the overstay rate for Mexicans and Central Americans fell somewhat and the rate for all other nationals remained constant.[56] The resulting estimate, that 41 percent of unauthorized migrants were visa overstayers in 2005, is identical to the result for 1997. Most recently, Warren updated his estimates of the overstay population and concluded that increased security measures following the 9/11 terrorist attacks dramatically reduced the number of overstays. From 2000 to 2009, new overstays dropped by 78 percent in the fifteen states that had the most overstays in 2000.[57]

Since 1997, it has been possible to estimate net change in visa overstayers using Warren's approach. Since 2004, the US-VISIT system—which records entry data for airline arrivals electronically—has also made it possible to match electronic entry data with airline passenger manifest data collected through another DHS program, the Arrival and Departure Information System (ADIS).[58] One effort by DHS to match US-VISIT entry records with ADIS departure records suggests that estimates of the overstay population may be inflated. In May 2011, DHS secretary Janet Napolitano ordered an investigation into nearly

1.7 million records of individuals thought to have overstayed since the introduction of US-VISIT. The review determined that more than half of those had actually left the country or had adjusted status and were living in the United States legally.[59] DHS is in the final stages of linking together entry-exit data with U.S. immigration databases, which will allow for much faster determinations of likely overstays. The department is currently making such determinations for all new visa and visa waiver travelers to the United States and plans in the near future to publish an overstay rate for each foreign country. The consequences for overstay are also increasing, because this information is shared with the State Department and could result in the traveler's visa being revoked.

The land borders remain the biggest challenge in identifying overstays. Exits across the northern border are recorded by the Canadian border authority, and the U.S. and Canadian governments have recently agreed to exchange entry and exit data and are doing so through initial pilot projects. The goal is to share entry and exit data for all border crossings, for Americans and Canadians as well as third-country nationals.[60] The southwest land border will soon constitute the sole major issue in visa overstay estimation. The United States and Mexico may be able to negotiate information-sharing arrangements regarding third-country nationals and visa travelers, though infrastructure and data systems remain inadequate at many Mexican ports of entry. This would leave entries and exits on Border Crossing Cards (BCCs), which are used by citizens of Mexico for short-term stays in the border region, as the one remaining challenge for visa overstay estimation. The recording of BCC entries is done electronically, using cards with biometric identifiers, but a huge number of entries is made every year and exits are not tracked.[61] Estimates of the total flow of visa overstayers may thus be sensitive to the estimate of BCC overstayers, and some way of verifying exit of BCC entries needs to be developed, most likely through information-sharing.[62]

EFFECTIVENESS OF ENFORCEMENT IN THE INTERIOR

Interior enforcement of U.S. immigration laws has two main components. First, workplace verification and employer sanctions are designed to discourage employers from hiring unauthorized workers. The goal is to deter would-be illegal migrants by making it difficult for them to find employment—what is often called "turning off the jobs magnet." Second, efforts to identify, arrest, and remove those without authorization are designed to make unauthorized migrants less certain that they will be able to continue living and working in the United States. The goal is to encourage unauthorized migrants to return home—a strategy that has been dubbed both "attrition through enforcement" and "self-deportation"—and to dissuade future would-be illegal migrants.

Better worksite enforcement has long been considered the linchpin for reducing illegal immigration, on the reasonable assumption that if unauthorized migrants cannot find work, they will not come to the United States. Federal efforts at curbing job opportunities for unauthorized migrants, though, have largely failed to date. Additionally, analytical work that attempts to understand the relative effectiveness of workplace enforcement versus border enforcement in increasing behind-the-border deterrence has been limited.

The central recommendation of the Select Commission on Immigration and Refugee Policy established by Congress in 1978 was that employers who knowingly hired unauthorized immigrants should be charged with a criminal offense. The recommendation became the centerpiece of the 1986 reform act. IRCA left unresolved the question of identity documents, however, and few resources were dedicated to workplace enforcement in the years following its passage. Employers were simply required to record the documents used to verify status, but not to attest to the authenticity of those documents. Fraud therefore became widespread. In 1996, Congress created the Basic Pilot, a voluntary system to assist employers in proving workplace eligibility. The system allowed employers to check new hires directly against government Social Security records and immigration databases to determine employment eligibility. In 2007, the administration of President George W. Bush renamed this system E-Verify and set about improving the accuracy of the system and encouraging voluntary use by employers. E-Verify was later made mandatory for federal government contractors and is now required for many companies in nineteen states. Still, fewer than 10 percent of the roughly seven million employers in the United States are currently using the system.

The tools for policing compliance by employers have also evolved. Under the 1986 scheme, employers have generally been immune from prosecution if they can show a good faith effort at compliance. Under the George W. Bush administration, an effort was made to focus on egregious violations through workplace raids, which often resulted in the arrest and removal of those unauthorized workers as well as criminal charges for identity fraud. Under the Obama administration, the focus shifted to workplace audits, which have resulted primarily in monetary fines and other penalties against employers shown to have hired significant numbers of unauthorized migrants. How effective these measures are at deterring illegal entry is unknown.

Nor have there been analytical studies that look at the deterrent effect of Secure Communities or other programs that increased federal-state cooperation in identifying unauthorized migrants, particularly those with criminal records, and placing them in removal proceedings. Launched by the federal government in 2008, Secure Communities has now been implemented in nearly all jails and prisons in the United States. The program screens those arrested against criminal and immigration databases, and in FY2011 accounted for about 20 percent of removals.[63] In theory, it should be possible to track recidivism rates among those identified and deported through Secure Communities, and over time to build evidence as to the effectiveness of this and other removal programs in discouraging illegal reentry.

The MMFRP surveys of Mexican migrants have found that interior enforcement—which includes worksite verification, workplace raids, and local police collaboration with ICE—has increased fear among unauthorized Mexican migrants living in the United States, making them scared to drive, use public transport, or go to a hospital. The surveys, though, have found no behind-the-border deterrent effect: individuals report that fear of workplace raids or arrest and removal had no bearing on their migration decisions. In the most recent survey, most respondents in the Mexican sending communities reported that it was still easy for unauthorized workers to find jobs; 25 percent said they were asked for no documentation.[64]

The recent increase in the number of states that have mandated the use of E-Verify for employers has allowed for something of a natural experiment of the effectiveness of workplace enforcement. Sarah Bohn and her colleagues examined the consequences of Arizona's 2007 Legal Arizona Worker Act (LAWA), one of the first and most far-reaching of these efforts.[65] LAWA requires all employers in the state to enroll in the E-Verify system and imposes harsh sanctions on employers who knowingly hire illegal immigrants, including suspension of a business license on a second offense. In the two years following its enactment, LAWA appears to have had a significant effect on the number of unauthorized residents in Arizona. The population of noncitizen Hispanic immigrants, which is presumed to include large numbers of unauthorized immigrants, fell by 17 percent—ninety-two thousand persons—in 2008 and 2009 because of LAWA. The law also appears to have pushed more individuals into self-employment or the informal economy. Extrapolating these results to a national scale is difficult, however, because many of the unauthorized migrants presumably relocated to other U.S. states where the laws remain less stringent.

In a 2009 report, Lawrence Wein, Yifan Liu, and Arik Motskin developed a discrete-choice model that assesses the probability that a migrant will choose an illegal path based on the likelihood of success at the border (the probability of apprehension), the likelihood of removal after successful entry to the United States, and the U.S. wage for unauthorized workers, which is affected both by worksite enforcement and by the number of legal, low-skilled immigrants.[66] The authors acknowledged that their model of worksite enforcement was insufficiently developed to reach any definitive conclusions. Their research suggests, though, that additional workplace enforcement was roughly twice as cost-effective as additional border enforcement in increasing deterrence. In their model, increased worksite enforcement reduces the wages of unauthorized workers, because employers pass on the risk of being caught and paying fines to their workers in the form of reduced compensation. Those lower wages then reduce the incentive to migrate illegally. In a 2012 Homeland Security Institute report, Joseph Chang, Alison Reilly, and Dean Judson developed this model further and used it to carry out various simulations related to enforcement strategies against illegal migration.[67] Analytical tools that use an integrated framework such as that of Wein, Liu, and Motskin are essential for evaluating the cost-effectiveness of alternative enforcement strategies.

HAS ENFORCEMENT DETERRED ILLEGAL IMMIGRATION?

Law enforcement reduces violations of the law in two primary ways: stopping violations during the planning or in the act, and deterring violations from occurring in the first place. No obvious consensus has been reached among U.S. immigration experts on the level of deterrence created by enforcement, and the empirical study of enforcement effects on illegal immigration has been limited.

A recent report of the National Research Council concludes that "studies of behavior generally show that rising enforcement has little deterrent effect on undocumented immigration" and that "rather than acting as a deterrent, increased enforcement appears to have other effects on migrant behavior: it increases the duration of trips and reduces the likelihood of return migration; it shifts border crossing away from concentrated areas of enforcement; and it increases the likelihood of crossing with a border smuggler."[68] A report by the same organization released a year later concludes that "studies of migration tend to find evidence of small but significant deterrent effects of border enforcement."[69] Empirical analysis of law enforcement specifically for unauthorized migrants is lacking, but empirical studies of law enforcement more broadly show significant deterrent effects on illegal behavior.[70]

To determine whether a potential migrant is deterred, data are needed on potential migrants who decided to migrate and those who decided not to, and on the various factors potentially influencing their decision. Such analysis is challenging to carry out in terms of data availability and technical issues.[71] The most recent research on deterrence has been conducted by Scott Borger, Gordon Hanson, and Bryan Roberts, who use data from the Mexican national household survey for 2002 to 2010.[72] They identified individuals who migrated from Mexico and those who did not, developed measures of economic prospects in the United States and in Mexico, assessed U.S. border enforcement and the ease of migrating legally, and estimated the degree to which these factors affected whether an individual decided to migrate illegally in this period.[73] Preliminary results suggest that the Great Recession, improvements in the Mexican economy, and border enforcement intensification were all significant influences on the downturn in illegal immigration since 2003, and that each of these factors may have accounted for roughly one-third of the downturn. Expansion of legal channels for temporary entry to work—in particular, the increasing use of the H-2A farmworkers visa program—also played a role. These results suggest that enforcement in recent years has had a more significant effect than previous research concluded.[74]

Policy Implications and Recommendations

Designing better policies for the future will be difficult unless lawmakers have a better grasp on the effectiveness of immigration enforcement in reducing illegal immigration to the United States. Three recommendations are especially important:

- First, the U.S. government should measure important enforcement outcomes and report on them in a timely fashion.
- Second, the evidence derived from this data needs to be used by Congress and the administration to make regular adjustments to the different tools that can be used to influence illegal immigration levels.
- Third, Congress should use this evidence to weigh alternative approaches that may be equally or more effective than enforcement in reducing illegal immigration.

WHAT SHOULD THE U.S. GOVERNMENT MEASURE AND REPORT ON ILLEGAL IMMIGRATION OUTCOMES?

The primary outcomes of law enforcement activity and, therefore, outcome performance measures for law enforcement organizations, are the rates at which the laws under their jurisdiction are broken. For U.S. immigration law, the primary measures are the rate at which individuals enter and live in the country unlawfully.

A full performance measurement framework should also have supporting measures and analyses. These include the number of apprehensions and the apprehension rate, along with the consequences of apprehension. The level of deterrence created depends on these variables. This analysis can be challenging and may require disentangling interrelated effects, such as the effect of law enforcement and economic changes on illegal immigration flows. It is necessary for effective management, however. A large empirical literature in the legal and economics fields examines deterrence effects in law enforcement more broadly, but not immigration law enforcement specifically.

Although the immigration bureaucracy has collected and reported a large volume of statistical data since its inception in the late 1800s, it does not currently report the critical elements of a coherent performance management framework, even though the Government Performance and Results Act (GPRA), first enacted in 1993, requires this (see Table 4).

GPRA and its recent reissue as the GPRA Modernization Act, seek to make federal agencies more accountable for results, in part through reporting performance measures, which are quantified results related to inputs, outputs, and outcomes. Inputs are the resources that agencies expend in their operations and are the easiest to measure. Outputs are immediate results of agency programs and are also frequently relatively easy to measure and report. Outcomes are related to the ultimate goals of what agency programs are trying to achieve. Agencies are required by law to report performance measures to the public and do so in annual performance and accountability reports. In the case of illegal immigration, an example of an input measure would be the number of Border Patrol agents deployed to the southwest border; an example of an output measure would be the number of apprehensions made by those agents and the apprehension rate; and an example of an outcome measure would be the number of successful illegal entrants.

The U.S. government reports substantial information about inputs into the illegal-immigration enforcement process. Indeed, most of the public debate about border security has been about inputs—whether the United States has enough Border Patrol agents, enough surveillance, enough fencing. To take one of many possible examples, President Obama said in a notable speech on immigration in El Paso in May 2011, "The Border Patrol has 20,000 agents—more than twice as many as there were in 2004. . . . We tripled the number of intelligence analysts working at the border. I've deployed unmanned aerial vehicles to patrol the skies from Texas to California." Citing such achievements, the president said that "we have strengthened border security beyond what many believed was possible." The government does not report most outputs, however, nor does it report outcomes. Research and evidence suggest that, if the government chose to do so, it could report meaningful information on several outputs and outcomes today, and

TABLE 4. PERFORMANCE REPORTING AT DHS

Outcome	Performance Measures	FY11 Annual Performance Report[a]
Illegal entry between ports	number of attempted illegal entries	none
	number of apprehensions	partial
	apprehension rate	none
	number of successful entries	none
Illegal entry at ports	number of illegal entries	none
	number of apprehensions[b]	none
	apprehension rate	none
	number of successful illegal entries	none
Visa overstay	number of new visa overstayers	none
Illegal immigrants resident in the United States	number of illegal immigrants resident in the United States[b]	none
Voluntary departure	number of illegal immigrants leaving of their own accord	none
Law enforcement removal	number of illegal migrants removed	partial
Deaths and adjustments	number of illegal immigrants who died or became legal	none
Legal immigration	number of new H2A and H2B visas issued[b]	none

[a]This column indicates whether the performance measure was reported by DHS in its FY2011–2013 Annual Performance Report.

[b]Although not reported in the DHS Annual Performance Report, some data on these measures are available from other sources

Source: Authors' calculations based on DHS's FY2011–2013 Annual Performance Report.

that it could report on additional and better outputs and outcomes after making resource investments that would be quite small in comparison with agency budgets.

This lack of transparency and accountability has not always been the case. After struggling to define missions and performance measures after GPRA was passed in 1993, the Department of Justice launched a major effort in 2001 to publish meaningful performance measures on illegal immigration and illegal drugs. In its 2002 annual performance report, the department gave the unauthorized immigration population resident in the United States and the gross inflow of unauthorized immigrants as official departmental performance measures and published both historical values and future targets for them.[75] When the immigration bureaucracy was moved to the newly formed DHS in 2004, however, the measures that had been reported in 2002 and 2003 ceased to be publicly reported. In 2005, DHS began to report a new measure related to border control, the "number of miles of the southwest border under effective control." This measure was reported annually through 2010, when it too was removed. DHS secretary Napolitano has said that "operational control," as the measure was known, was not an accurate reflection of the effectiveness of enforcement at U.S. land borders, and has promised to offer alternate measures.

It is widely recognized that to be acceptable, performance measures should meet certain criteria:

- Measures should be *meaningful*, clear, and readily *understandable* by the audiences that will consume them.[76]
- The data should be *valid*, not systematically biased or distorted. In particular, data should not be subject to observer bias or systematic over- or underreporting.
- Collection of data should be *reliable*, consistent, and uniform over time and across reporting units.
- Results should be *timely and actionable*—that is, available such that they are useful to informing decisions and resource allocation.
- An agency's set of performance measures should provide a *balanced and comprehensive* performance picture.

The unauthorized stock and inflow measures that were briefly reported in 2002 and 2003 met these criteria. The measure that replaced them, the "number of miles of the southwest border under effective control," did not. The levels of control to which a mile of border was assigned did not have obvious interpretations. The designation of control level for a particular mile was ultimately based on the subjective assessments of Border Patrol leadership, and outside parties could neither replicate this process nor attest to its validity.[77] It was not clear that collection and processing of data related to determining a border mile's status was consistent and uniform over time and across reporting units (specifically, Border Patrol stations).

INS and subsequently DHS have thus clearly been capable of pro-
ducing measures that meet the criteria for properly measuring performance. Although resistance by public-sector agencies to measuring
stocks and flows that are not directly observable has traditionally been
fierce, INS did initiate and support efforts to measure the unauthorized
population and stock of visa overstayers from the 1980s onward, and it
briefly reported quality performance measures on illegal immigration
in the early 2000s.[78] USCG also reported the interdiction rate for illegal migrants at sea. Since the early 2000s, however, performance measure reporting has slipped rather than progressed.

The government agency to which Congress turns to provide oversight on agency performance, the Government Accountability Office
(GAO), has also had a mixed record in promoting improvements. In
the 1990s, GAO was active in evaluating existing data and estimates
and promoting progress in measuring outcomes. A 1993 GAO report
reviewed existing data and estimates related to illegal immigration
stocks and flows.[79] In 1997, GAO produced a major report on the border
enforcement intensification strategy of the late 1990s that considered
in depth the measurement challenges related to evaluating control of
illegal immigration and the many potential sources of data that could be
used to construct measures.[80] This report's main conclusion is worth
citing in full:

> Although developing a formal evaluation plan and implement-
> ing a rigorous and comprehensive evaluation of the strategy may
> prove to be both difficult and potentially costly, without such an
> evaluation the Attorney General and Congress will have no way
> of knowing whether the billions of dollars invested in reducing
> illegal immigration have produced the intended results. Devel-
> oping a formal evaluation plan would be in keeping with the con-
> cepts embodied in the Government Performance and Results Act
> of 1993 (the Results Act) to develop evaluations and performance
> measures to gauge whether the goals and objectives are being
> achieved. Although, in response to the Results Act, the Justice
> Department's draft strategic plan described some specific pro-
> gram goals, strategies, and performance indicators, it did not con-
> tain an evaluation component to explain how the Department will
> assess success in meeting these goals or, more broadly, the effec-
> tiveness of the southwest border strategy. A formal evaluation

plan would assist Justice in identifying whether INS is implementing the strategy as planned, what aspects of the strategy are most effective, and, if the strategy's goals are not being achieved, the reasons they are not. Such information would help the agency and Congress identify whether changes are needed in the strategy, in policy, in resource levels, or in program management.[81]

GAO then issued a report in 1999 that stated proper measures of illegal immigration outcomes were still lacking.[82] But in subsequent reports in 2003 and 2008, the lack of proper measures was not mentioned. Then a 2011 report used the "miles under control" measure without questioning it or commenting on the lack of outcome measures. The most recent report reviews in depth the Border Patrol's known-flow data, which is reported in this study, and shows a welcome shift back to the view of the 1990s when GAO was evaluating actual immigration enforcement outcome measures and data.[83]

The extra cost involved in developing good outcome measures for illegal immigration would be quite small in comparison with agency budgets. Expenditures of $2 million a year would amount to 0.06 percent of the 2012 budget requested by the U.S. Border Patrol but, if properly targeted and spent, could significantly enhance data required to improve existing estimates. Simply integrating existing administrative record databases collected by the various immigration enforcement agencies and making them available to external researchers would lead to major advances. This step would require commitment and determined leadership from top officials at DHS but would have minimal budgetary implications.[84]

Whether the U.S. government will report meaningful measures on illegal immigration outcomes ultimately depends on whether political leadership wants them. Performance measures in the federal government are remarkably unstable. They can and have been changed at the will of political leadership, and agencies and offices that are supposed to act as guardians and gatekeepers often seem reluctant to exercise oversight. Given the significant public controversy over illegal immigration, the need for objective measures and analysis has long been clear, but since the early 2000s the federal government has had a great deal of difficulty in responding to it.

Congress should make the development and reporting of such performance measurement mandatory and tie it to future appropriations as part of any immigration reform legislation. At a minimum, the outcome measures required by the Government Performance and Results Act should be included as reporting requirements (see Table 4). In addition, a comprehensive research agenda should be sponsored that analyzes the effects of outputs and inputs on law enforcement outcomes.

HOW SHOULD PERFORMANCE DATA BE USED IN THE ONGOING MANAGEMENT OF ILLEGAL IMMIGRATION?

The use of data to drive law enforcement strategy and execution has become standard in many local police departments. New York City pioneered the effort in 1994 with its crime statistics database, Comp-Stat, which requires precinct commanders to report statistics for all crimes on a weekly basis.[85] The results are compared with crime statistics over previous periods, and that data is shared in real time with the public.

The Department of Homeland Security and other agencies with responsibility for immigration enforcement, such as the Department of Justice and the State Department, need the same kind of data-driven revolution. Performance measures should also be used to identify problem areas and develop effective responses.

Accurate and timely measures of gross inflows by sector would be extremely valuable in deployment decisions for scarce border enforcement resources. The Border Patrol could develop the capacity to redirect manpower and technology into sectors along the southwest border experiencing unexpectedly high levels of illegal inflow or to step up the use of consequences programs in those sectors. Better estimates of illegal flows through ports of entry would allow DHS to weigh the relative merits of additional Border Patrol personnel versus additional port inspectors. The lion's share of the funding in recent years has gone to the Border Patrol, on the assumption that its area of responsibility between the ports of entry posed the greatest risks. The result has been less investment at the ports of entry, increased waiting times, and higher costs for legal commerce and legal cross-border travelers.

Visa overstays are another area where significant progress is possible. Regular collection and reporting of overstay data would allow the government to identify worrisome trends. A spike in overstays from a particular country, for example, would lead to extra scrutiny by State Department consular officers on other visa applicants from that country. Better data could lead to still more targeted responses. If the overstays, for instance, are concentrated among travelers from certain regions of the country, or in particular occupations, consular officers would have still better tools for determining risks among future visa applicants.

Regular measurements and reporting of important outcomes would have further value in focusing the often highly contentious debate over immigration and encouraging fact-based choices between alternative goals and strategies. For instance, although many in Congress have long favored better border security in general terms, only recently has the debate begun to focus on what a secure border actually means.[86]

Some have argued that the border should be "sealed" against illegal entry; indeed, the Secure Fence Act of 2006 directed the DHS secretary to achieve "operational control" of the border, which the act defined as "the prevention of all unlawful entries into the U.S., including entries by terrorists, unlawful aliens, instruments of terrorism, narcotics, and other contraband." Sealing the border requires that the probability of apprehension be so high, and consequences for being caught so severe, that almost complete deterrence of attempted illegal entry is achieved. East Germany achieved a 95 percent probability of apprehension in the late 1970s by intense deployment of enforcement resources and imposition of severe consequences, including shoot-to-kill orders for border guards. This experience suggests that current resources for the U.S. Border Patrol would need to increase by a minimum of a factor of three to achieve such deterrence, and almost certainly by more than this, given the restrictions under which agents operate. A Border Patrol force of a hundred thousand agents with significantly more infrastructure and equipment than they now have might be able to effectively seal the border (see Appendix 4 online).[87]

A similar debate could be had over workplace and interior enforcement, though the evidence is less developed. The risks an undocumented migrant in the interior faces seem to be significantly less than those associated with border crossing, and increasing them substantially would require higher enforcement expenditure than current levels.

What outcome resulting from interior enforcement would be analogous to sealing the border? Several can be imagined. First, the probability of obtaining employment could be driven to zero. This would presumably require making the E-Verify program mandatory for all U.S. employers and reengineering the program so that it results in more deterrence and better supports other enforcement activities.[88] However, this will expand the informal employment sector, and the ability to be employed in this sector can be reduced only through other enforcement actions. Measures will also have to be undertaken to mitigate identity theft in ways that are not seen as impinging unnecessarily on privacy.

Second, the probability of being deported could be driven to near 100 percent. Increasing the deportation rate would carry exorbitant resource, human, and political costs. In a 2005 Center for American Progress report, Rajeev Goyle and David Jaeger developed a cost estimate for an effort to deport all illegal residents and found that, based on conservative assumptions, it would be at least $206 billion over five years.[89] The additional resources required to increase the probability of deportation significantly above its current level, but far below a level of 100 percent, are not clear but presumably would require a major expansion of the enforcement budget.

The availability of such measures is especially important when budgetary resources are scarce, which is likely to be the situation confronting the Department of Homeland Security and other government agencies for many years. For the first decade of its existence, Congress threw so much money at DHS that it was rarely forced to weigh costs against benefits and make difficult decisions on resource deployment. That is no longer the case. Better reporting of outcome measures would help lawmakers make more effective resource allocation decisions.

As it did for crime in New York City, moving to a data-driven management system for immigration law enforcement will require political commitment. This commitment will need to occur in both the executive and legislative branches of the federal government. Congressional oversight needs to be strengthened to maintain focus on successful management of illegal migration. Relevant committees in Congress should hold regular, perhaps quarterly, hearings to review forecasts, examine trends in outcome performance measures, and assess DHS proposals for adjustments to its strategies as conditions on the ground change. To assist in this effort, Congress should direct DHS to establish an early warning system that monitors the outcome performance measures identified earlier, along with economic, demographic, law enforcement, and other trends that may affect these outcomes. This system should include both the monitoring of relevant measures and the analytic ability to forecast them.

ALTERNATIVES TO ENFORCEMENT FOR CONTROLLING ILLEGAL IMMIGRATION?

Consider the following thought experiment. If the United States were to remove all quotas on legal immigration, the problem of illegal immigration would disappear overnight. By definition, anyone with the wherewithal to board a plane or take a bus and arrive in the United States would be a legal resident. There would be no need for any form of immigration enforcement. Consider the converse. If the United States were to eliminate all legal immigration, the problem of illegal immigration would become orders of magnitude larger. The government would need to implement a far bigger immigration enforcement effort simply to keep down the number of unauthorized migrants.

Neither of these extremes is plausible, of course, but they underscore the interconnected nature of any effort at reforming U.S. immigration laws. Larger legal programs, particularly for unskilled workers who have few legal alternatives for coming to the United States, would likely reduce illegal immigration. One of the many lessons from the failure of the 1986 IRCA was that the absence of a legal immigration path for most unskilled Mexicans and Central Americans was probably a significant contributor to the surge in unauthorized migration in the 1990s.

IRCA was in some ways the least optimal policy conceivable for deterring illegal migration. It coupled weak enforcement at the workplace and at the border with strict quotas on unskilled workers that allowed few legal options for migration.

A different experiment occurred in 1954 and had two elements at its core: a significant increase in legal entry through the Bracero program coupled with an extensive enforcement operation that increased the cost of illegal entry, known as Operation Wetback. Bracero admissions reached over four hundred thousand at their peak in the mid-1950s (see Figure 1). Illegal entry fell significantly until the mid-1960s, when the Bracero program was abolished because of rising concerns over poor wages and working conditions for migrants.

Even though the Bracero program was intended to accommodate the increased demand for Mexican labor that World War II had brought about, illegal immigration rose in the mid-1940s and accelerated through the early 1950s for several reasons. First, it was often easier and cheaper for American farms to employ illegal immigrant workers than to use the Bracero program. Second, the program quota was probably significantly less than the demand from growers. Finally, the U.S. Border Patrol was underfunded and unprepared; from 1942 to 1951, apprehensions rose by over 400 percent, yet Border Patrol personnel fell by 30 percent.[90] Labor demands rose again when the Korean War broke out in 1950. Even though the Bracero quota had been increased to two hundred thousand by the early 1950s, Border Patrol apprehensions exceeded the quota by two to four times (see Figure 1).[91]

In 1953, the magnitude of illegal immigration from Mexico and other concerns led the new Eisenhower administration to tackle the problem. The new strategy relied on both enforcement and expansion of the Bracero program. A large-scale enforcement operation was carried out in the summer of 1954 that coordinated federal, state, and local law enforcement to sweep regions at the border and in the interior and either move illegal migrant workers into the Bracero program or remove them from U.S. territory. The Bracero quota was also doubled to over four hundred thousand and maintained at this level through the late 1950s. Illegal immigration fell to low levels from 1956 to 1965. In 1960, the documentary *Harvest of Shame* was shown on U.S. television. The show illustrated the plight of American migrant farm workers and created pressures to end the program. The Kennedy administration lowered the Bracero quota steadily in the early 1960s, and the program was finally eliminated in 1965. Illegal immigration immediately began to climb. Bracero, of course, is not a model for a modern temporary-worker program. Nor can it be definitively stated based on the available evidence that guest-worker programs are preferable to expanded permanent immigration quotas in reducing illegal migration. But the experience of the 1950s indicates that both tougher enforcement and expanded legal migration options can work together to reduce illegal migration significantly.

In an ideal world, the United States would run pilot experiments using different legal admission schemes and different enforcement schemes, and then assess their effect on the inflow of unauthorized migrants and other indicators. Such experiments are unlikely. The bottom line is that successful management requires an understanding of what works and what does not. To improve the management of immigration law enforcement, DHS should begin systematically evaluating the effects of existing programs, implement detailed program evaluation plans for all new programs, and make systematic use of pilot programs and other experimental methods to identify what works and what does not in reducing illegal immigration.

SUMMARY OF RECOMMENDATIONS

- Congress should direct the development and reporting of performance measures identified in Table 4 and tie performance to future appropriations, as part of any immigration reform legislation. In addition, a comprehensive research agenda should be sponsored that analyzes the effects of inputs and outputs on law enforcement outcomes. DHS should be estimating empirically the effects of different enforcement activities on illegal immigration flows.

- To facilitate better ongoing management of illegal immigration, Congress should direct the Department of Homeland Security to establish an early warning system that monitors outcome performance measures along with economic, demographic, law enforcement, and other trends that may affect these outcomes. This should include both the monitoring of relevant measures and the analytic ability to forecast them.

- DHS should begin sponsoring systematic modeling of illegal immigration trends and develop forecast models of illegal immigration flows and stock. This could be directed as part of immigration reform legislation as a necessary step in monitoring implementation and adjusting policies as the environment changes. No empirical modeling and monitoring of trends will provide perfect forecasts, but policymakers should not have to operate without analytical information.

- Congressional oversight should be strengthened to maintain focus on successful management of illegal migration. Relevant committees in Congress should hold regular, perhaps quarterly, hearings to review the early warning system data and forecasts, examine trends in outcome performance measures, and assess DHS proposals for adjustments to its strategies as conditions change.

- To gain a better understanding of the effectiveness of law enforcement activities and tools, Congress should direct DHS to systematically undertake program evaluation analysis that measures the effectiveness of individual programs. All new programs should include an evaluation plan that identifies program measures, data collection methods, and evaluation milestones. To strengthen congressional oversight, program evaluation results should be provided to Congress and discussions of program evaluation results and implications should be included in regular oversight hearings.

- The Obama administration should release its enforcement data to outside researchers. Full release of apprehension record data, in particular would enable a great deal of research that would create better understanding of the characteristics and size of illegal flow across the southwest border, the effect of economic and enforcement factors on this flow, and other important topics. DHS should also recruit and support internal researchers, encourage them to work on these issues and interact with academic researchers, and approve their work for public dissemination.

Conclusion

The scale of government activities to enforce legal migration and deter illegal migration has become enormous over the past two decades, but the data available to assess the effectiveness of these activities is distressingly sparse. The recent buildup in law enforcement likely has had a significant positive effect on illegal immigration outcomes, but the magnitude of those effects and the utility of different enforcement tools remain difficult to assess. Better data and analyses—to assist lawmakers in crafting more successful policies and to assist administration officials in implementing those policies—are long overdue.

Endnotes

1. Doris Meissner, Donald M. Kerwin, Muzaffar Chishti, and Claire Bergeron, "Immigration Enforcement in the United States: The Rise of a Formidable Machinery," Migration Policy Institute, 2013.
2. Mike Lillis, "Hill Poll: Voters oppose deportations, but see border as vulnerable," *The Hill*, February 4, 2013, http://thehill.com/polls/280775-hill-poll-voters-oppose-deportations-but-see-border-as-vulnerable.
3. Marc R. Rosenblum, "What Would a Secure Border Look Like?" Testimony to the House Committee on Homeland Security, Subcommittee on Border and Maritime Security, February 26, 2013.
4. U.S. Border Patrol, "Border Patrol Strategic Plan: 1994 and Beyond," July 1994, p. 6.
5. The focus in this report is on controlling the borders of the United States with respect to illegal migration. It does not address questions such as the level and composition of legal immigration and what to do about the large undocumented population currently resident in the United States. Furthermore, it is focused on the large-scale economic migration that accounts for most illegal entries, particularly across the southwest land border, and does not focus on terrorist and criminal (for example, drug smuggling) migrants. Although all of these issues are also important, they are beyond the scope of this report.
6. The unauthorized population is estimated using the residual methodology, in which an estimate of the size of the legal immigrant population is subtracted from the estimated foreign-born population. For more information, see Frank D. Bean, R. Corona, R. Tuiran, and Karen A. Woodrow-Lafield, "The Quantification of Migration Between Mexico and the United States," *Migration Between Mexico and the United States, Bi-National Study*, vol. 1, 1998, pp. 1–90. For a history of the development of this methodology and an accessible review of estimates, see Ruth Ellen Wasem, "Unauthorized Aliens Residing in the United States: Estimates Since 1986," Congressional Research Service report 7-5700. The authors used the estimate of two million from Robert Warren and Jeffrey S. Passel, "A Count of the Uncountable: Estimates of Undocumented Aliens Counted in the 1980 United States Census," *Demography*, vol. 24, no. 3, 1987, pp. 375–93. Estimates for 1986 and 1988 are from Karen A. Woodrow and Jeffrey S. Passel, "Post-IRCA Undocumented Immigration to the United States: An Assessment Based on the June 1988 CPS," in Frank D. Bean, Barry Edmonston, and Jeffrey S. Passel, eds., *Undocumented Migration to the United States: IRCA and the Experience of the 1980s* (Washington, DC, and Santa Monica, CA: Urban Institute Press and RAND Corporation, 1990). Estimates for 1990 to 2000 are based on the 2000 census and are taken from Robert Warren, "Estimates of the Unauthorized Immigrant Population Residing in the United States: 1990 to 2000," Office of Policy and Planning, U.S. Immigration and Naturalization Service, 2000. Estimates for 2000 to 2010 are from Passel, D'Vera, and Gonzeles-Barrera, "Net

Migration," and Jeffrey Passel and D'Vera Cohn, "Unauthorized Immigrant Population: National and State Trends, 2010," *Pew Research Center*, February 1, 2011. Estimates by the DHS Office of Immigration Statistics for 2000 through 2010 are based on the 2000 census and are from Michael Hoefer, Nancy Rytina, and Bryan Baker, "Estimates of the Unauthorized Immigrant Population Residing in the United States: January 2010," Office of Immigration Statistics, Policy Directorate, U.S. Department of Homeland Security, 2011. Estimates for 2010 and 2011 are based on the 2010 census and are from Michael Hoefer, Nancy Rytina, and Bryan Baker, "Estimates of the Unauthorized Immigrant Population Residing in the United States: January 2011," Office of Immigration Statistics, Policy Directorate, U.S. Department of Homeland Security, 2012. Recent estimates from Robert Warren and John Robert Warren, "Unauthorized Immigration to the United States: Annual Estimates and Components of Change, by State, 1990 to 2010," *International Migration Review*, Spring 2013, are particularly useful because they reconcile estimates based on the 1990, 2000, and 2010 censuses. Figure 3 shows how estimates of the unauthorized and the foreign-born populations for a particular year can change after a new decennial census becomes available: estimates based on projecting forward from a census conducted in year X contain projection errors that can be corrected once a census for year X+10 is available.

7. Estimates of the Mexican foreign-born population resident in the United States are from Jeffrey S. Passel, Cohn D'Vera, and Ana Gonzeles-Barrera, "Net Migration from Mexico Falls to Zero—and Perhaps Less," Pew Hispanic Center Report, April 23, 2012.

8. Other legislation related to illegal immigration has also been passed in the last two decades, including the Illegal Immigration Reform and Immigrant Responsibility Act of 1996, which increased penalties for illegal presence in the United States, established a pilot workplace verification system, and authorized an increase in the Border Patrol to ten thousand agents; the Antiterrorism and Effective Death Penalty Act of 1996, which tightened asylum rules and increased penalties for immigration-related offenses; the USA Patriot Act of 2001, which strengthened background checks on visa applicants and tracking of foreign students; and the Secure Fence Act of 2006, which authorized seven hundred miles of fencing along the Mexican border, increased use of surveillance technologies, increased the number of Border Patrol agents, and mandated the expansion of detention facilities in the interior.

9. The literature in demography, economics, and sociology that analyzes illegal migration from Mexico and other Latin American countries to the United States is enormous. Important references consulted for this study that can provide more extensive references to this literature include the following: Gordon H. Hanson, "Illegal Immigration from Mexico to the United States," *Journal of Economic Literature*, vol. 44, 2006, pp. 869–924; Wayne A. Cornelius and Jessa M. Lewis, *Impacts of Border Enforcement on Mexican Migration* (San Diego: Center for Comparative Immigration Studies, 2007); Cornelius, David Fitzgerald, Jorge Hernandez-Diaz, and Scott Borger, *Migration from the Mexican Mixteca* (San Diego: Center for Comparative Immigration Studies, 2009); Cornelius, Fitzgerald, Hernandez-Diaz, and Borger, *Four Generations of Norteños* (San Diego: Center for Comparative Immigration Studies, 2009); Cornelius, Fitzgerald, Pedro Lewin Fischer, and Leah Muse-Orlinoff, *Mexican Migration and the U.S. Economic Crisis* (San Diego: Center for Comparative Immigration Studies, 2010); Steve Redburn, Peter Reuter, and Malay Majmundar, eds., *Budgeting for Immigration Enforcement: A Path to Better Performance* (Washington, DC: National Academies Press, 2011); Alicia Carriquiry and Malay Majmundar, eds., *Options for Estimating Illegal Entries at the U.S.-Mexico Border* (Washington, DC: National Academies Press, 2012). The website of the Mexican Migration Project (http://mmp.opr.princeton.edu) also provides references to the extensive literature that uses data from this survey.

10. The interdisciplinary literature on migration in the social sciences is large, and different disciplines have tended to emphasize the importance of different influences. For an in-depth review, see Caroline B. Brettell and James F. Hollifield, *Migration Theory: Talking Across Disciplines* (New York: Routledge, 2000). However, convergence among these disciplines has been substantial in recent years on the nature of the individual decision to migrate and the dynamics of mass migration. Economists fully recognize the importance of social networks in explaining migration. For an example of an embedded social network in an economic rational-choice model of migration and resulting "snowball" dynamics, see William J. Carrington, Enrica Detragiache, and Tara Vishwanath, "Migration with Endogenous Moving Costs," *American Economic Review*, vol. 86, no. 4, 1996, pp. 909–30. Empirical studies by economists of the Mexico-U.S. migration flow now routinely include variables that capture the influence of social networks. See also Cornelius et al., *Four Generations of Norteños*, pp. 1–41. Also, for a review of influences on migration dynamics in the context of the Mexico-U.S. migration flow, see Douglas S. Massey and Kristin E. Espinosa, "What's Driving Mexico-U.S. Migration? A Theoretical, Empirical, and Policy Analysis," *American Journal of Sociology*, vol. 102, no. 4, 1997, pp. 939–99.

11. See Michael Clemens, Claudio E. Montenegro, and Lant Pritchett, "The Place Premium: Wage Differences for Identical Workers across the U.S. Border," Center for Global Development Working Paper No. 148, July 2008. They find that differences in wages for immigrants in the United States and what they could have earned in their home countries are much greater than international differences in the prices of goods or returns on investments, as well as wage differentials inside countries.

12. The level of migration is influenced by the costs and benefits to the immigrant of migrating, including the legal barriers to immigration and the degree to which they are enforced. For an analysis of the influences on migration of Europeans to the New World from 1850 to 1914, see Timothy J. Hatton and Jeffrey G. Williamson, *The Age of Mass Migration: Causes and Economic Impact* (Oxford: Oxford University Press, 1998). For an analysis of the influence of economic and policy factors on legal migration to the United States from 1971 to 1998, see Ximena Clark, Timothy J. Hatton, and Jeffrey G. Williamson, "Explaining U.S. Immigration, 1971–1998," *Review of Economics and Statistics*, vol. 89, no. 2, 2007, pp. 359–73.

13. In all of these comparisons, an important issue arises. It is necessary to convert a wage that could be earned in Mexico in pesos into U.S. dollars so that it can be compared with a potential U.S. wage. Two exchange rates can be used to make this conversion: the commercial rate at which people actually exchange pesos for dollars and the PPP rate. The commercial rate is determined in foreign exchange markets by actual trading of currencies. The PPP rate is the ratio of the cost of a standardized basket of goods and services in Mexico in pesos to the cost in the United States in dollars. The PPP rate is thus used to compare the standard of living of someone resident in the United States with that of someone resident in Mexico. If the wage ratio is calculated using the PPP rate, it captures the gain that a potential migrant would enjoy if he or she were to remain in the United States permanently. If the wage ratio is calculated using the commercial exchange rate, however, it captures the gain to a migrant who works in the United States and then returns to Mexico and spends most of his or her U.S. earnings in Mexico. The former ratio is the more relevant comparison for a temporary or circular migrant who does not plan to live in the United States on a long-term basis, whereas the latter ratio is more relevant for a migrant who is contemplating a permanent change. The wage gap will be smaller if calculated using the PPP rate and larger if calculated using the commercial rate. See Appendix 1 at www.cfr.org/illegal_immigration_report.

14. Clemens, Montenegro, and Pritchett, "The Place Premium." The authors only provide wage gap estimates using the PPP exchange rate. We use the ratio of the commercial exchange rate to the PPP exchange rate for Mexico in 2000 (1.55) to obtain a value of 3.9. It is important that they do not evaluate the wage gap for particular individuals based on what they have actually earned or perceive they could earn in their home country and destination country; rather, they estimate using 2000 U.S. census data and average wages earned by people with the same observable characteristics in other countries using household survey data, and make a ratio of these two wages. Unobservable characteristics that could cause this wage gap to overstate how much wages really differ are possible. In particular, many believe that immigrants are a special group that has higher-than-average "pluck," or entrepreneurial drive, a quality that cannot be directly observed. The authors are able to control for the pluck factor for several countries, including Mexico; they find that the U.S.-Mexico wage gap is essentially unaltered.

15. Other studies do not find evidence that wage gaps are converging. See Raymond Robertson, "Has NAFTA Increased Labor Market Integration Between the United States and Mexico?" *World Bank Review*, vol. 19, 2005, pp. 425–48; and David Gandolfini, Timothy Halliday, and Raymond Robertson, "Globalization and Wage Convergence: Mexico and the United States," working draft, 2013. The latter study uses household survey and census data and finds that long-run wage differences of matched age-education cohorts show little change. When wage convergence is observed, the convergence seems to be driven by a drop in the wages of less-educated and younger U.S. workers rather than wage gains in Mexico. It also seems that for cohorts differentiated by migration probabilities, wage differentials drive migration rather than migration driving wage differentials.

16. Academic research on the U.S.-Mexico income gap has focused on the period since 1960 and has found evidence of periods when the income gap has fallen and when it has risen. After careful statistical analysis of the income gap calculated using the PPP exchange rate, William Easterly and his colleagues concluded in a 2003 report (William Easterly, Norbert Fiess, and Daniel Lederman, "NAFTA and Convergence in North America: High Expectations, Big Events, Little Time," *Economia*, vol. 4, no. 1, 2003, pp. 1–53) that the gap will converge in the long run to a value of roughly two. Interestingly, the spike in the PPP income gap during World War II suggests a dramatic (although temporary) increase in the incentive for Mexican workers to come to the United States at that time.

17. This gap was powerfully affected in the short term by major changes in the dollar-peso commercial exchange rate, including the two crises in Mexico in 1987 and 1994.

18. The current-dollar income ratio in the 1960-to-2010 span is regressed against a linear time trend, and the regression results are used to linearly extrapolate the ratio forward in time. This simplistic exercise does not explicitly model how the wage gap is determined.

19. Recent experience presents an actual example of Americans taking advantage of such an opportunity. Many Americans were willing to work as contractors in war zones in Iraq and Afghanistan in order to double or triple their income in the 2000s.

20. All historical and projection data presented in this section are from the database for *World Population Prospects: The 2010 Revision*, Population Division of the Department of Economic and Social Affairs, United Nations.

21. A simple linear regression of apprehensions on population was used to estimate the historical relationship and make predictions.

22. See Gordon H. Hanson and Craig McIntosh, "The Great Mexican Emigration," *Review of Economics and Statistics*, vol. 92, no. 4, 2007, pp. 798–810, for a careful

analysis of net emigration from Mexico from 1960 to 2000. The authors conclude that labor-supply shocks accounted for 40 percent of Mexican labor flows to the United States. Their research may offer a basis for a framework in which scenarios for future flows can be analyzed.

23. Underfunding of the U.S. Border Patrol through the 1980s is documented in Kitty Calavita, *Inside the State: The Bracero Program, Immigration, and the I.N.S.* (New York: Routledge, 1992) and is discussed later in this report,

24. Marc R. Rosenblum, "Border Security: Immigration Enforcement Between Ports of Entry," Congressional Research Service, January 6, 2012.

25. This section draws on the research of Doris Meissner et al., "Immigration Enforcement in the United States."

26. See Government Accounting Office, "Illegal Aliens: Despite Data Limitations, Current Methods Provide Better Population Estimates," GAO/PEMD-93-25, 1993, p. 4. The report states that "the GAO found that using INS apprehensions data as a proxy for the inflow of illegal aliens is problematic. A drop in the number recorded may result from fewer entry attempts because aliens are remaining here for longer periods, fewer persons are actually attempting entry, or the U.S. Border Patrol is less productive or has fewer resources with which to operate." Also see Henry H. Willis, Joel B. Predd, Paul K. Davis, and Wayne P. Brown, "Measuring the Effectiveness of Border Security Between Ports-of-Entry," RAND Technical Report, 2010. The authors provide evidence that a fall in apprehensions has been cited by immigration enforcement authorities as reflecting enforcement success due to deterrence, and a rise in apprehensions as success due to a higher probability of apprehension.

27. For an extensive review of migrant and household surveys and their ability to support estimation of illegal entries at the U.S.-Mexico border, see Alicia Carriquiry and Malay Majmundar, eds., *Options for Estimating Illegal Entries at the U.S.-Mexico Border* (Washington, DC: National Academy of Sciences, 2012). Also see Appendix 3 online for a more extensive discussion of migrant and household surveys.

28. The weight on attempted crossings at ports is relatively small, as a minority of trips is attempted at ports.

29. Since the mid-2000s, all non-Mexican nationals have been detained after apprehension and repatriated to their home country. This creates a very high level of at-the-border deterrence, which greatly complicates the underlying model that recidivism analysis is based on with respect to non-Mexicans, who now account for more than one-quarter of Border Patrol apprehensions.

30. Recent evidence from a new sensor system deployed in the Tucson sector in 2012 (the VADER system) suggests that in the 150-square-mile area that it covered, the probability of apprehension was roughly 50 percent, which is consistent with the survey and recidivism evidence. This rate is not a border-wide measure, but it was measured in one of the busier entry corridors on the southwest border. See Brian Bennett, "Radar shows U.S. border security gaps," *Los Angeles Times*, April 3, 2013.

31. See Government Accountability Office, "Key Elements of New Strategic Plan Not Yet in Place to Inform Border Security Status and Resource Needs," GAO 13-25, 2012. We calculate the known-flow probability of apprehension as the ratio of apprehensions to apprehensions plus got-aways.

32. See, for example, a study prepared by Michael McCaul, "A Line in the Sand: Confronting the Threat at the Southwest Border," the Majority Staff of the House Committee on Homeland Security, 2010. It reported that "federal law enforcement estimates that 10 percent to 30 percent of illegal aliens are actually apprehended."

33. Estimates of the probability of apprehension can be combined with the total apprehensions of Mexican nationals in the southwest border region to produce

estimates of the total successful entries using the mathematics of the repeat-trials process. Estimates based on the recidivism methodology are sensitive to the rate of at-the-border deterrence, but those based on migrant survey data are not. Gross inflow levels in the 1980s and 1990s implied by MMP data are much higher than those implied by MMFRP data. Borger showed that MMP-based estimates of gross inflow are not consistent with estimates of the unauthorized population based on the residual methodology, but that MMFRP-based estimates are (see Appendix 3 online for details). This is an important point, because it suggests that the probability of apprehension is significantly higher than suggested by the MMP data. Although the MMP- and MMFRP-based estimates are quite different before the 2000s, these estimates and the recidivism-based estimates converge in the 2000s. All three show a significant fall in gross inflow after 2001. In 2010 and 2011, the MMP-based flow estimate rises dramatically, due to the sharp fall in estimated probability of apprehension in these two years. However, MMP has observations on only seven illegal migration trips in 2010 and two in 2011. Probability of apprehension estimates for these two years are likely to change significantly as more data on illegal migrations in these years are collected over time. Finally, known-flow data on got-aways suggests that by 2011, successful entries were below one hundred thousand, which is substantially less than what the other methodologies suggest.

34. The gross inflow estimates from 1979 to 2009 are derived from two migrant surveys, the Mexican Migration Project (MMP) and the Migration Field Research Program (MMFRP). Estimates for the 2001-to-2010 period are based on recidivism analysis and are under the assumptions that at-the-border deterrence equals 0 percent or 20 percent. They also include the implied probability of apprehension based on known-flow data recorded by the Border Patrol on the southwest border. As discussed more extensively in Appendix 3 online, the MMP-based estimates of the probability of apprehension in the 1990s may be too low, given the wording of the MMP survey questionnaire.

35. Adding an estimate of non-Mexican-national inflow to the estimates of Mexican-national inflow would increase them, but not greatly. Apprehensions of non-Mexican nationals peaked at roughly one hundred thousand in the mid-2000s and have fallen substantially since then.

36. Given the small MMP sample size for illegal migration trips in these years, the level of the deterrence rate is subject to some uncertainty, but it is unlikely that the rise is a small-sample artifact.

37. The annual number of apprehensions at ports on the southwest border was in the tens of thousands in the late 2000s, which is low compared with those made between the ports. The sheer volume of entry processing at many ports on the southwest border may present challenges for record keeping. There is an inherent tension between the goals of facilitating lawful travel and commerce and preventing unlawful entry.

38. It is also not clear whether the COMPEX program includes randomized inspections of entry documents in addition to vehicles. Entry on false documents is a potentially significant component of overall illegal entries and includes those entering on foot (pedestrians) as well as in vehicles.

39. The MMP survey unfortunately does not ask migrants whether they entered at a port or between the ports.

40. For a review of issues related to achieving both of these missions, see Government Accountability Office, "Vulnerabilities and Inefficiencies in the Inspections Process," GAO-03-1084R, August 18, 2003.

41. The interdiction rate reported through 2007 was measured as the ratio of the sum of interdictions and deterred potential migrants to the sum of interdictions, deterred potential migrants, and illegal migrant arrivals. The number of illegal migrant arrivals

by sea is the value of known flow minus interdictions, where known flow is estimated by the USCG and other relevant agencies and governments based on interdiction activities, surveillance, and intelligence. The number of potential illegal migrants is an estimate of how many migrants would have attempted illegal entry in the absence of enforcement operations and is thus equivalent to a measure of behind-the-border deterrence discussed more extensively in the land context later in this report.

42. USCG also reported the interdiction rate of cocaine at sea from 1995 through 2009. This measure was also removed from public reporting in 2010.

43. For a history of illegal migration estimates through 1990, see Edmonston, Passel, and Bean, "Perceptions and Estimates of Undocumented Migration to the United States," in Bean, Edmonston, and Passel, *Undocumented Migration.* Also, for additional detail on early estimates, see Kenneth Hill, "Immigration Policy: Past to Present," in Daniel B. Levine, Kenneth Hill, and Robert Warren, eds., *Immigration Statistics: A Story of Neglect* (Washington, DC: National Academy Press, 1985).

44. The chance of being removed equals the number of DHS removals divided by the mid-year size of the unauthorized population.

45. See, for example, Warren and Passel, "A Count of the Uncountable"; Woodrow and Passel, "Post-IRCA Undocumented Immigration"; Bean et al., "The Quantification of Migration"; Warren, "Estimates of the Unauthorized Immigrant Population Residing in the United States: 1990 to 2000"; Jeffrey Passel and D'Vera Cohn, "U.S. Unauthorized Immigration Flows Are Down Sharply Since Mid-Decade," *Pew Research Center*, September 1, 2010; Hoefer, Rytina, and Baker, "Estimates of the Unauthorized Immigrant Population Residing in the United States: January 2010"; Wasem, "Unauthorized Aliens"; and Warren and Warren, "Unauthorized Immigration to the United States."

46. Unreasonable levels of undercount are required in order for estimates of the unauthorized population to significantly understate its true value. Nonetheless, even given this and the fact that estimates of this population enjoy more credibility than any other measurement made today with respect to illegal immigration outcomes, "estimates" that are based on assertion and/or misguided analysis continue to appear and enter into the public debate. See Robert Justich and Betty Ng, "The Underground Labor Force Is Rising to the Surface," Bear Stearns Asset Management, January 3, 2005. They claim that the unauthorized population was twenty million rather than twelve million. Although the analysis of the memo does not withstand careful scrutiny, the twenty million figure was widely cited by some prominent media figures for several years after the memo was published.

47. In December 2001, Senator Carl Levin testified to a treasury subcommittee that his staff had attempted to find data on the percentage of those assigned court dates who actually showed up for their hearing. He testified, "The INS wasn't able to tell us how many of the persons arrested in this situation and released fail to show up for their scheduled hearing. However, by looking at related statistics and ballpark estimates, we estimated that the number is at least 40 percent and possibly as high as 90 percent," http://www.levin.senate.gov/newsroom/press/release/?id=896ac451-d492-4322-bd78-a802a1e55ead.

48. The number of inadmissibles is recorded by CBP's Office of Field Operations, which manages the ports of entry. This number includes those refused entry at land border crossings, airports, and seaports. Inadmissible numbers are not provided before 2005. It is thus not entirely clear whether inadmissibles include those who attempt entry at a port while concealed in a vehicle. For discussion and review of DHS data on enforcement actions, see John Simanski and Lesley M. Sapp, "Immigration

Enforcement Actions: 2011," annual report, Office of Immigration Statistics, Department of Homeland Security, 2012.

49. Redburn, Reuter, and Majmundar, *Budgeting for Immigration Enforcement*. The authors provide data that is roughly equivalent to this ratio and arrive at this conclusion (see Figure 4-2 and discussion on pp. 48–49).

50. This approach implicitly assumes that all inadmissibles are subject to return, which is probably not the case. It also assumes that no ICE apprehensions are subject to return, which is probably close to the truth.

51. Redburn, Reuter, and Jajmundar, *Budgeting for Immigration Enforcement*, p. 50.

52. Cornelius et al., *Mexican Migration and the U.S. Economic Crisis*. Due to limitations of data on criminal activity in Mexico, it has not been possible to incorporate these risks into studies of deterrence. See Scott Borger, Gordon Hanson, and Bryan Roberts, "The Decision to Emigrate From Mexico," presentation at 2012 Society of Government Economists annual conference, Washington, DC, 2012.

53. See Robert Warren, "Annual Estimates of Nonimmigrant Overstays in the United States: 1985 to 1988," in Bean, Edmonston, and Passel, *Undocumented Migration*.

54. The Government Accountability Office (GAO) contributed constructive recommendations that Warren incorporated into his estimation procedures. For details, see Government Accountability Office, "Illegal Immigration: INS Overstay Estimation Methods Need Improvement," GAO/PEMD-95-20, 1995.

55. For a discussion of the DHS estimates and a review of the measurement challenges with respect to Canadian and Mexican entries, see Government Accountability Office "Overstay Tracking: A Key Component of Homeland Security and a Layered Defense," GAO-04-82, 2004.

56. Pew Hispanic Center, "Modes of Entry for the Unauthorized Migrant Population," Fact Sheet, May 22, 2006.

57. Robert Warren and John Robert Warren, "A Review of the Declining Numbers of Visa Overstays in the U.S. from 2000 to 2009," Center for Migration Studies, 2013.

58. As in I-94 stub matching, system error will be associated with this approach, but such error is presumably less than for paper stub matching, and it should be possible to develop correction factors.

59. See Edward Alden and Bryan Roberts, "Are U.S. Borders Secure? Why We Don't Know, and How to Find Out," *Foreign Affairs*, July/August 2011; John Cohen, "Ten Years After 9/11: Can Terrorists Still Exploit Our Visa System?" testimony by principal deputy coordinator for counterterrorism at DHS, House Homeland Security Subcommittee on Border and Maritime Security, September 12, 2011.

60. The current U.S.-Canada Beyond the Border initiative calls for the two countries to "share United States–Canada entry data at the land border such that the entry information from one country could constitute the exit information from another through an integrated entry and exit system." See Department of Homeland Security, "United States-Canada Beyond the Border: A Shared Vision for Perimeter Security and Economic Competitiveness," Action Plan, December 2011.

61. Pew Hispanic Center, "Modes of Entry." It cites 148 million entries on border crossing cards in 2004.

62. One approach would be to give a random sample of those entering on BCCs a paper form with an exit stub that is collected on departure and then determine overstay rates for the sample. Those in the sample could be given incentives to return exit stubs through threat of sanction if exit is not verified. It should also be noted that those entering on nonimmigrant visas may adjust their status to another nonimmigrant visa or an immigrant visa while in the United States, or extend the period of their visa. Controlling for this presumably requires matching of entry records to records in databases that record changes in status and visa extensions.

63. Meissner et al., "Immigration Enforcement in the United States."
64. Cornelius et al., *Mexican Migration and the U.S. Economic Crisis.*
65. Sarah Bohn, Magnus Lofstrom, and Steven Raphael, "Did the 2007 Legal Arizona Workers Act Reduce the State's Unauthorized Immigrant Population?" IZA Discussion Paper No. 5682, April 2011.
66. Lawrence M. Wein, Yifan Liu, and Arik Motskin, "Analyzing the Homeland Security of the U.S.-Mexico Border," *Risk Analysis*, vol. 29, no. 5, 2009, pp. 699–713.
67. Joseph C. Chang, Alison Reilly, and Dean Judson, "A Unified Model of the Illegal Migration System," Homeland Security Institute, 2012.
68. See Redburn, Reuter, and Majmundar, *Budgeting for Immigration Enforcement*, p. 34.
69. See Alicia Carriquiry and Malay Majmundar, *Options for Estimating Illegal Entries at the U.S.-Mexico Border*, pp. 2–13. This study provides references to several research studies that quantify effects of enforcement on the decision to migrate illegally to the United States.
70. For a comprehensive review of empirical studies of crime, see Steven Levitt and Thomas Miles, "Empirical Study of Criminal Punishment," in A. Mitchell Polinsky and Steven Shavell, eds., *Handbook of Law and Economics*, vol. 1 (North Holland, 2007).
71. Passel, D'Vera, and Gonzeles-Barrera show that the proportion of repatriated unauthorized migrants surveyed in the EMIF-N migrant survey stating that they will never return to the United States rose from 7 percent to 20 percent between 2007 and 2010 ("Net Migration," pp. 24–26). Although this evidence is suggestive that deterrence has risen, it is based on statements of intentions rather than observation of actual choice.
72. Borger, Hanson, and Roberts, "The Decision to Emigrate from Mexico."
73. The research is not able to take into account some influences on the decision to migrate, including the risk of being raped, extorted, or murdered by smugglers. Enforcement intensity is also measured using data on Border Patrol manpower. There are many other enforcement inputs used by the Border Patrol, and enforcement at the ports and in the interior may also have affected illegal immigration flows, but data on these enforcement variables over time are not available.
74. The research has not yet been finalized due to the authors losing access to internal DHS apprehension record data in mid-2012. Researchers need data from individual apprehension records maintained by DHS in order to properly analyze illegal immigration into the United States. DHS has publicly disseminated all data needed by researchers from these records except the "fingerprint identification number," which is the number assigned to records for the same individual as determined from examination of fingerprints. The fingerprint identification number is what permits recidivism analysis to be carried out. As this number is an arbitrary designation and cannot be used to identify an individual, reasons for not disseminating this information to the researcher community are unclear. For additional discussion on the need for DHS to provide more extensive access to administrative record data, see Carriquiry and Majmundar, *Options for Estimating Illegal Entries.*
75. These measures were published at what turned out to be the peak of the illegal immigration wave.
76. See Theodore H. Poister, "Performance Measurement: Monitoring Program Outcomes," in Joseph S. Wholey, Harry P. Hatry, and Kathryn E. Newcomer, eds., *Handbook of Practical Program Evaluation* (San Francisco: Jossey-Bass, 2010) for best practices in performance measurement of program outcomes.
77. Although this assessment was ultimately subjective, Border Patrol officers did take into account data on criminal activity and other factors when making their assessments.
78. This resistance was documented as early as 1985: "The pessimistic views that the illegal alien population, being a clandestine population, is essentially unsurveyable

and that reasonable data on it may never become available have affected attitudes to data collection, data use, and data evaluation since illegal aliens reemerged as an issue in the early 1970s to the recent discussion of legalization and control issues in the Simpson-Mazzoli legislation. Results of imaginative data collection and analysis projects carried out over the last few years have not been given the credence they deserve because of the belief that the uncountable cannot be counted" (Levine, Hill, and Warren, *Immigration Statistics*, p. 225). Estimates of the unauthorized population now enjoy widespread credibility in spite of this resistance, which continues to affect and impede measurement of other outcomes associated with illegal immigration.

79. Government Accounting Office, "Illegal Aliens."

80. The Government Accountability Office lists "indicators for measuring the effectiveness of the strategy to deter illegal entry along the southwest border." These include recidivism analysis, known-flow estimation, estimation of the probability of apprehension from migrant survey data, and estimated number of illegal entry attempts at the ports of entry. "Illegal Immigration: Southwest Border Strategy Results Inconclusive; More Evaluation Needed," GAO-98-21, 1997, pp. 80–91.

81. Ibid, p. 5.

82. This report noted that INS had contracted with a private firm to "design an evaluation strategy, identify data needs and analytical approaches, and conduct a study of the southwest border strategy." Government Accountability Office, "Illegal Immigration: Status of Southwest Border Implementation," GAO-99-44, 1999, p. 26.

83. Government Accountability Office, "Key Elements of New Strategic Plan Not Yet in Place to Inform Border Security Status and Resource Needs," GAO-13-25, 2012.

84. Carriquiry and Majmundar, *Options for Estimating Illegal Entries.* They strongly advocate for greater provision of information from DHS to external researchers, better collaboration of DHS with this community, and integration of internal administrative datasets of CBP and ICE.

85. For a more detailed discussion, see John Whitley, "Five Methods for Measuring Unobserved Events: A Case Study of Federal Law Enforcement," IBM Center for Business and Government, 2012.

86. For a more detailed discussion of the definition of border security, see Alden and Roberts, "Are U.S. Borders Secure?"

87. Resources of the enforcement agency that administers ports of entry would also have to increase significantly. Less information on enforcement outcomes is available for ports of entry in the U.S. and the East German case, and this prevents doing a similar benchmarking exercise for the ports. See Appendix 4 at www.cfr.org/illegal_immigration_report.

88. The effectiveness of the E-Verify program in accurately determining immigration status is an important issue. A program review suggests that because of identity theft, E-Verify identifies only roughly 50 percent of unauthorized potential hires. See Westat, "Findings of the E-Verify Program Evaluation," report submitted to U.S. Department of Homeland Security, 2009.

89. Rajeev Goyle and David A. Jaeger, "Deporting the Undocumented: A Cost Assessment," Center for American Progress, July 2005.

90. See Calavita, *Inside the State.*

91. Interestingly, one action undertaken after 1947 was to legalize illegal migrant workers found by enforcement authorities and move them into the Bracero program. See Calavita, *Inside the State*, pp. 28–29.

About the Authors

Bryan Roberts is a senior economist at Econometrica, Inc. He was previously a senior economist at Nathan Associates. He is also an adjunct lecturer at George Washington University's Trachtenberg School of Public Policy and Public Administration. Roberts was previously the assistant director for border and immigration issues of the Office of Program Analysis and Evaluation at the Department of Homeland Security (DHS). He also worked in DHS's Office of Policy and Science and Technology Directorate as an economist and program manager, analyzing issues related to risk analysis, border security, immigration, nonimmigrant travel and trade, and other homeland security areas. Before working at DHS, Roberts was as an economic adviser in several countries of the former Soviet Union and the Balkans. Roberts holds a BA from the University of Pennsylvania and a PhD in economics from the Massachusetts Institute of Technology.

Edward Alden is the Bernard L. Schwartz senior fellow at the Council on Foreign Relations, specializing in U.S. economic competitiveness. Alden also directs the CFR Renewing America publication series. The former Washington bureau chief for the *Financial Times*, his work focuses on immigration and visa policy and on U.S. trade and international economic policy. He is the author of the book *The Closing of the American Border: Terrorism, Immigration, and Security Since 9/11*, which was named a 2009 finalist for the J. Anthony Lukas Book Prize for nonfiction writing. Alden was the project director of the 2009 CFR-sponsored Independent Task Force on U.S. Immigration Policy, which was chaired by former Florida governor Jeb Bush and former White House chief of staff Thomas "Mack" McLarty. Alden was previously the Canadian bureau chief for the *Financial Times*, based in Toronto, and before that was a reporter at the *Vancouver Sun*, specializing in labor and employment issues. He also worked as the managing editor of the newsletter *Inside U.S. Trade*. He holds a BA in political science from the University of British Columbia and an MA in international relations from the University of California, Berkeley, and he pursued doctoral studies before returning to a journalism career.

John Whitley is an economist who studies resource allocation and performance issues in national security. He is also an adjunct lecturer at George Washington University's Trachtenberg School of Public Policy and Public Administration. He previously served as the director of the Office of Program Analysis and Evaluation (PA&E) at the Department of Homeland Security, where he led the DHS resource allocation process and the measurement, reporting, and improvement of performance. Before DHS, Whitley worked in the Department of Defense's Office of PA&E on defense resource allocation issues, the U.S. Senate, and academia, and served in the U.S. Army. Whitley holds a BA from Virginia Tech and an MA and a PhD in economics from the University of Chicago.